THE POETRY OF LUIS CERNUDA

PQ 6605 .E7 A6 1971
Cernuda, Luis.
The poetry of Luis Cernuda.

THE POETRY OF LUIS CERNUDA

Edited by

Anthony Edkins & Derek Harris

New York University Press

New York 1971

WITHDRAWN

RITTER LIBRARY
BALDWIN-WALLACE COLLEGE

Permission to quote Cernuda's poetry in Spanish has been granted by Sr. Dr. Don Angel Maria Yanguas Cernuda, as Literary Executor for the Estate of Luis Cernuda, and the original publishers of the Works in Spanish, Fonda de Cultura Economica, Mexico City, Mexico. All correspondence concerning permissions to quote any and all English language material in this volume should be addressed to the publishers, New York University Press, Washington Square, New York 10003.

Copyright © 1971 by New York University
Library of Congress Catalogue Card Number: 74-173878
ISBN: 0-8147-2151-6
Manufactured in the United States of America

Preface

Today Luis Cernuda (1902-1963) is widely recognized as one of the major Spanish poets of this century, but only within the last decade has his work begun to receive the attention it deserves. He belonged to that brilliant group of poets, who include Federico García Lorca, Jorge Guillén, Pedro Salinas and Rafael Alberti, poets who came into prominence in the 1920s and were then caught up in the holocaust of the Spanish Civil War. While many of his contemporaries had won acclaim before the Civil War, Cernuda had had an uneasy time with the critics, and his exile after the war in non-Spanish-speaking countries left him in an even deeper limbo than that of other exiles. But he had a small band of admirers, mainly fellow-poets in both Spain and Latin America, whose number gradually increased until the appearance of an edition of his collected poems in 1958 made his work available to a larger audience. Now his poetry is exercising a significant influence on the new generation of Spanish poets.

His poems express a tragic view of life as an unequal conflict between personal aspiration and objective reality, summed up in the title he gave to his collected work, *Reality and Desire*. He was obsessed by a dream of a perfect existence where reality and desire were one, where the division between self and world was obliterated, and he sought in a variety of ways to make this dream come true. This often gives to his poetry a strongly evasive character, since when faced with a reality hostile to his dreams he frequently attempted to retreat into his private realm of desire rather than compromise the dream. But this is not a sign of an effete personality, that fragile "man of glass" several critics have tried to make of him. As the successive attempts to realise the dream failed one by one, he used these experiences of failure to teach himself to come to terms with the gulf between that dream of a perfect existence and the imperfect reality in which he had to exist. He came finally to understand that the dream itself was merely a pretext, a vehicle for self-affirmation. *Reality and Desire* is Cernuda's emotional and spiritual autobiography from adolescence to old age, the poetic record of his search for his personal truth, and of his determination when he had found that truth to be true to it. Yet it is more than the story of a man learning to live with himself, for the Luis Cernuda who appears in the poems is a transfigured personality. The passionate, almost destructive integrity with which he searched for his truth makes him an exemplary poet. The struggle to assume and sustain an ethic responsibility for his own life provides a mirror for the human condition.

The translations gathered together here are the first attempt to put before an English-speaking audience a representative selection of Cernuda's poems. Examples are provided of his work at every major phase of its development in an effort to present a cross-section of his poetry which will contain the more important facets of his complex character. This has been the main criterion of selection, although the choice has been, in part, determined by which poems were available in translation. The introduction gives a general guide to Cernuda's work and offers a reading of the poems selected.

Although four separate translators have contributed to this volume, they have, in general, shared a common approach to the problems of translating poetry. The aim has been to keep the translation as close to the Spanish text as is consistent with producing a fluent English version. The translations can stand alone, but are presented here beside the originals, so that the reader with a little knowledge of the language can use the English versions as a means of access to the Spanish poems.

Three of Edward M. Wilson's translations ("Lazarus," "Urban Cemetery" and "Impression of Exile") were done in consultation with Luis Cernuda and approved by him. Edward M. Wilson also wishes to acknowledge the help he received from the late John Crow, formerly of King's College, London. "Impression of Exile" was previously published in the *Times Literary Supplement* and "Gulls in the Parks" in *The Cambridge Review*. "Nevada" and "A wound does not make a dead man" have appeared in *Gong* (Nottingham, England), "Cobwebs Are Hanging from the Mind" in *West Coast Review*, and "Before Leaving" in *Quartet*.

The Poetry of Luis Cernuda

The single volume of verse entitled *Reality and Desire*, into which Cernuda gathered his poems, is a complex work made up of eleven separate collections of poems spanning a period of nearly forty years from 1924 to 1962. Despite its complexity this work has the organic unity of life itself, since it is Cernuda's autobiography, and it is held together even more firmly by the central theme of conflict between reality and desire. This conflict between the objective and subjective dimensions of life was first formulated in precise terms in an essay written in 1935:

> I was drawn by desire towards the reality that lay before my eyes as if it were only by its possession that I could become convinced that I existed. But since I have never achieved such possession, except precariously, there followed a movement in the opposite direction: hostility to the deceptive attraction of reality. Since, as it appears, this or a similar experience has also been felt by some philosophers and poets whom I admire, I, like them, believe that external reality is a mirage and the only certain thing is my own desire to possess it. Thus, the secret essence of poetry, as I see it, resides in the conflict between reality and desire, between appearance and truth, which permits us to gain a glimpse of that complete picture of the world of which we are unaware.

Cernuda carried throughout his life the dream of transcendent existence where he would be able to enter into harmonious communion with the world. This led him into a succession of evasive attitudes as he tried to escape his sense of estrangement, yet the experience of estrangement was his reality, the reality with which he was ultimately forced to come to terms. Moreover, the key element in the statement quoted above is the idea that the desire to possess the world sprang from his need to affirm his own existence. This existential quality of the conflict between reality and desire, clearly seen by him in 1935, was, in effect, the fundamental motivating force of his poetry. His poems are the means by which he sought to discover and sustain his identity in an indifferent or hostile environment that would diminish him.

For Cernuda the conflict between reality and desire embraced all facets of life, but it acquired sharpest focus in the context of the clash between his erotic desires and the harsh reality of love's experience. The erotic context also exposed most clearly the basic existential concern reflected in this conflict, which was made especially bitter and violent in this area by his homosexuality. Yet he was not a homosexual poet, but a homosexual *and* a poet. He used his personal experience to validate his poetry while transcending that personal experience through his poetry to make a statement of common human significance. As a homosexual he found his dreams and his identity most exposed to attack from a hostile environment, and this is part of his personal truth which cannot be ignored without betraying what Cernuda struggled to achieve in his poetry. His homosexuality must be recognized by the reader, as he accepted it himself, and it can then be seen as a metaphor for man's alienated condition in the world and in society.

Cernuda himself admitted that he possessed a complex, difficult character, and much of this complexity is reflected in the *persona* he created for himself in his poems. Widely differing, even contradictory attitudes could exist side by side as the struggle between reality and desire provoked conflicting emotional and intellectual responses. Something of the variety of his responses is expressed in one of his mature poems, "The Adoration of the Magi," included in this anthology. The four characters in this ambitious composition, the Three Kings and a shepherd who witnessed their journey, represent four different life-styles. Balthasar is a cynic who takes the world as he finds it, regardless of its injustice, Gaspar is a hedonist, concerned only for the voluptuous life, Melchior is a seeker of truth who scorns power and pleasure, while the shepherd is a simple man, untroubled by abstract ideas of truth, material possessions, sophisticated pleasures or the need for a religious faith, who lives in complete communion with the natural world around him. This shepherd lives what for Cernuda would be an ideal existence, but the characters of the Three Kings come closer to the reality of his experience.

The voice of Balthasar can be heard in the mood of tart petulance that sometimes entered his poems, Gaspar's life of sensual pleasure always held a fascination for him, and he shared Melchior's search for truth. There has been a strong tendency amongst Cernuda's critics to emphasise his peevish acerbity or his languor, "cold and alien, detached from life, disagreeable," as someone has described him. This strange image of a personality both astringent and indolent was rejected by Cernuda as a "legend," a falsification of his real personality. The dominant element of his character is the seeker of truth, just as Melchior is the dominant figure among the Kings in "The Adoration of the Magi," although as Cernuda pursued his own journey of experience he too was accompanied at every step by the cynic and the hedonist within him. The goal of Cernuda's journey, the dream of a perfect existence, proved to be as illusory as that sought by his Three Kings, but his journey did, nonetheless, enrich him with the experience he gained on the way until he came finally to realize that the goal itself was merely the stimulus for the journey.

Cernuda was born in Seville and lived there until 1928. His childhood and youth in this city, which even today has preserved much of its enchantment, left an indelible mark on his sensibility. There, in his adolescence, he first experienced the overwhelming desire to become one with the world, and there he had his first glimpse of that perfect existence where reality and desire coincide, although it also provided his first taste of bitterness when this proved to be no more than a glimpse. His early poems, contained in the collection *First Poems* (1924-1927), are a recreation of the ambivalent attitudes prompted by the adolescent experience of awakening to the world's promise only to find it beyond reach. These short poems in the post-symbolist manner use impressionistic descriptions of the poet's immediate environment—his room or the landscape seem from his window—to reflect mixed feelings of fervor and indolence. Fervor, a sense of potential happiness, is created by the adolescent's new perception of the world, while indolence results from his inability to translate this fervor into action. The adolescent protagonist of these poems is still innocent of the experience necessary to give him understanding of his new, unarticulated emotions. He lives in a twilight world of longing repressed by its own lack of substance. When he looks outside himself, as in the first poem of this selection, he finds a smiling landscape that seems to accept him and reflects his emotional awakening, but when he looks within himself at the shadowy world of nascent sexual desire, as in "Faithful sleep grants us," he finds a vacuum with nothing to reflect his dreams or give them life. However, in a moment of greater lucidity, in "I exist, well I know it," he rejects the only two dimensions his life knows at this time, the world outside and the restricting environment of his room, in favor of a dream of love. This is an important decision, a commitment to the erotic ideal when he is still unaware of the true nature of the world beyond the confines of his room, where that dream must seek fulfilment. But for the present all he can do is dream in solitude, although this can result in acute emotional claustrophobia, as in "Walls, nothing else." One solution for this sense of repression is to withdraw into a private world, a haven from oppressive, hostile reality, like the idyllic garden in "Hidden within walls," in whose propitious environment he can escape his feelings of alienation. The symbol of the hidden garden recurs throughout Cernuda's poetry as an expression of the persistent evasive tendency in his character. These poems, which deftly evoke the nebulous emotions of adolescence, record the creation of the dimension of desire and the first tentative conflict with reality.

The facile, uncomprehending criticism that greeted his first book in 1927 deeply hurt Cernuda, and perhaps partly as a result of this his next three collections were not published until 1936. *Eclogue, Elegy, Ode* (1927-1928) is a series of extensive poems in a classical style but continuing the adolescent thematic material of his first book as a gesture of scorn to his critics and an act of faith in himself. He was, however, dissatisfied himself with these longer poems because they failed to convey the intensified feelings of repression he was experiencing at this time, and no example from this series has been included in this selection.

At the end of 1928 Cernuda left Seville to spend six months in France, settling on his return in Madrid. The freedom he felt upon leaving his native city seems to have disappeared when he found himself confronted by an unyielding, alien reality that rejected his adolescent dreams. This change of circumstance seems also to have coincided with his recognition of his homosexuality and with a bitter experience of thwarted love. His reaction to the discovery of the reality he had not known before was a turmoil of anger, bewilderment and anguish. To find a vehicle for these violent, disturbed emotions Cernuda turned to Surrealism in the collection of poems he produced in 1929 called *A River, A Love*. The surrealist disregard of conscious logic enabled him to give voice to feelings so intense that they overwhelmed normal intellectual responses. Even so, he did not venture into automatic writing but used a technique of free-association to create poems that are powerful and strangely beautiful. Some poems, like "As the Wind," do remain in a more traditional mold, others are closer to the oneiric world of Surrealism, but all express a profound sense of dillusionment and an agonized feeling of alienation. The dream of love, however, had not been entirely destroyed; it continued to exist in distant terrestrial paradises given names like "Nevada," culled as *ready-mades* from the cinema and popular songs. Such—for Cernuda—exotic places were new versions of the hidden garden of his adolescence, havens from the inimical world in which he now felt trapped. Yet the very distance of the paradises are an indication of the erotic dream's disenchantment, and on occasions disillusion can even reach into some of these dream worlds, as in the Virginia of "Sea Flesh."

Forbidden Pleasures, Cernuda's next collection, was written largely in the space of a fortnight in April 1931, apparently as a result of another failure of his dream of love. These poems continue to use the surrealist technique of free-association, although the tone now tends to be calmer, sometimes even whimsical. This second failure of the dream was no longer such a shock and Cernuda could begin to seek for the cause of the failure. The delicate poem "Said Not a Word" concludes that one of the reasons was his own innocence which had made him search for an impossible ideal. But as he deepened his investigation of the dream's failure he saw that the primary cause was the hostility of society to the forbidden pleasures of his homosexuality, and to counter this he reconstructed the erotic ideal to place it beyond social contraint. The mood of wishful thinking in "If a Man Could Only Say" is turned to clear affirmation as sexual desire, likened to the sea, is declared to be a life-force of elemental proportions. Having given his desire the power to withstand social prohibition, Cernuda could return, in "Like a Slight Sound" to his old commitment to the dream of love. But now he could also see clearly the existential dimension in the erotic ideal, and the equation made in "If a Man Could Only Say" between desire and his personal truth marks the supremely important decision to accept his homosexuality as an essential part of himself. This refusal to compromise the dreams of desire with the demands of reality definitively turns the pursuit of love into a search for self-affirmation. Yet for the moment he could only remain lost in that alien, unreal world described with surrealistic appositeness in "I've Come to See", unreal because now the only true reality for him was the love missing in that world.

However, when Cernuda again found love it proved to be a sordid travesty of the transcendent experience for which he had hoped. This disastrous love affair was recorded in the collection *Where Oblivion Dwells* (1932-1933), where he moved away from surrealistic techniques, which had fulfilled their function of releasing his inhibitions, towards an evocative style influenced by the 19th-century Spanish poet Gustavo Adolfo Bécquer, with whose poems of tormented, disillusioned love he found a ready affinity. *Where Oblivion Dwells* is a work of violent disenchantment expressed with a deceptive calm that is a mask for cold despair. The loss of the love he had equated with life laid waste Cernuda's inner world of dreams and engulfed him in a spiritual death. The poem "I was" looks back to his adolescence and sees that all his youthful aspirations were futile, reduced now to total nullity. Yet desire continues, now a source of pain, since experience has shown that it can lead only to disaster. The solution offered is another form of escapism, a despairing escape into oblivion, into a perpetuation of that spiritual death created by love's failure, into an emotional numbness beyond the torment of dreams.

The bitter grief of *Where Oblivion Dwells* brings to an end a cycle of dream and disillusionment in Cernuda's early poems and leads him to a reassessment of his philosophy of life. It was in the aftermath of this experience of despair that he formulated the theory of the conflict between reality and desire, and of the existence of a hidden, transcendent world. This philosophical concern produced a change in emphasis in his poems from merely recording experience to analyzing it in a search for self-knowledge, and a stylistic change from the short song-type poems favoured in his early work to long, discursive compositions better suited to this new contemplative mood. His discovery at this time of the poetry of the German pre-Romantic Friedrich Hölderlin helped him find his new style and philosophy. In particular, the theme of the ancient gods, so characteristic of Hölderlin, was used by Cernuda to represent his belief in another, superior world which still preserved the poetic values of truth, beauty and justice that he had found were alien in the world of men. These new attitudes are first set out in the collection *Invocations* (1934-1935); "To the Statues of the Gods," the poem chosen from this collection, clearly shows the influence of Hölderlin and the condition of spiritual exile Cernuda adopted as a result of his poetic belief in the ancient gods. This belief, is, in effect, a further manifestation of the evasive attitude symbolized in the image of the hidden garden; the world of the gods is another dream, another haven from reality, another expression of Cernuda's alienation.

In 1936, reality, in the form of the Spanish Civil War, broke into this new dream. He sided with the cause of the Spanish Republic, although the elegiac style he had developed in *Invocations* helped him keep his poetry aloof from any direct political affiliation. He saw the war as a tragedy in which the Earth Mother Spain was torn apart by the fratricidal struggle of her sons. In 1938 he left Spain to go on a lecture tour of England on behalf of the Republican Government. Unknowingly, he was going into exile, for he never returned to Spain. His reactions to the war and to the first shock of exile are contained in the collection *The Clouds* (1937-1940). Cernuda felt the exile's inevitable sense of bitterness, accentuated by the contrast between the bleak, Nordic world that had given him asylum and the almost paradisiac vision of his childhood Andalusia that he now carried with him. He first settled in Scotland, in Glasgow, not a city noted for its beauty; the dismal townscapes of "Urban Cemetery" and "Gulls in the Parks" must have made a particularly painful contrast with his native Seville. The elegiac view of the past prompted by exile is the subject of the return to the hidden garden of adolescence in the poem "Old Garden," which is also deeply marked by the acute consciousness of time that he now acquired as he saw that his own youth had become another lost dream. Such backward looks into the past also indicate a sharpened concern with personal identity as exile confirmed in physical terms the spiritual alienation he had already experienced in Spain. The totally foreign environment that surrounded him appeared as lifeless to him as he felt himself. Even expressions of hope, as in the poem on the raising of Lazarus, which represents a brief attempt to find solace in Christianity, are scarred by a corrosive pessimism.

Yet exile was, paradoxically, a greatly enriching experience for Cernuda; by placing him in a completely alien setting it forced him to sustain himself by his inner strength alone, and it also caused him to pursue an already awakened interest in English poetry. Exile stimulated him to deepen his analysis of himself and opened to him the English tradition of meditative poetry which helped him in this task. Echoes of T. S. Eliot, for example, appear in "Impression of Exile" and "The Adoration of the Magi," while Robert Browning showed him how to project his experience onto historical or legendary characters such as Lazarus or the Three Kings. The use of the *doppelgänger* technique produced some of Cernuda's finest poems; he had a dramatic gift for accommodating language to character, and for creating characters who were both projections of himself and personalities in their own right. He now clearly saw the need to transcend his personal experience, believing with T. S. Eliot that the greater the distance between the man who suffers and the poet who creates the better the poem, and such objectivizing techniques enabled him to stand outside himself and gain the perspective required for the self-knowledge he now sought through his poetry. This self-contemplative intent also led him to a more colloquial expression where the rhythm of the phrase is deliberately set against the rhythm of the verse, focusing attention on the poem's content rather than its rhetoric.

The stimulus of exile brought Cernuda in his next collection, *Like Someone Waiting for the Dawn* (1941-1944), to one of the high points of his achievement. While still looking back with envy and regret at his lost youth, he now concerned himself even more firmly with turning over the past in his mind in order to understand the rôle it had played in fashioning his present self. The poem "The Family," frequently though unjustly cited as proof of Cernuda's astringency, is a good example of the technique of addressing himself in the second person, which he began to employ at this time as another means of gaining an objective viewpoint of his experience. The key-note of these poems is self-understanding, seen clearly in the contemplation of man's existence circumscribed by time in "The Ruins" and "The Hawthorns," which both conclude with the injunction to himself to learn to come to terms with the reality of life. "The Ruins," in particular, is an important poem for its rejection of any solace in supernatural belief and Cernuda's decision to stand alone with only the support of his poetry. He now understood that poetry was the source of his inner strength, the vehicle he used to discover himself, to affirm himself, to create himself. This is made plain in the systematic destruction of his illusions by the familiar demon in "A Man's Night with his Demon," one of Cernuda's finest poems, where the device of demonic temptation points directly at the ethic concern that now came to dominate his work. The demon first undermines the illusion of immortality Cernuda sought to find in his poetry, but has to abandon this line of attack when the man refuses to relinquish his commitment to poetry, which he sees as the last redoubt of his personal integrity. The demon then cruelly tempts the man with a vision of a "respectable" life, which is contemptuously rejected because it would be a denial of the man's truth. The poem ends on an ambivalent note of diffidence and stoic resignation, but in the penetrating self-analysis forced on him by his familiar demon Cernuda has spoken loud and clear with the voice of that seeker of truth who presided over his multi-faceted character. This confrontation with his devil's advocate is unequivocal evidence of Cernuda's resolve to keep faith with himself, that self he had discovered in the course of the rigorous analysis of his experience conducted in his poetry.

The consciousness of time overshadowing the poems of exile grew more acute in Cernuda's next two collections, *Living Without Being Alive* (1944-1949), begun in England and completed in Massachusetts, at Mount Holyoke College where he took up a teaching post in 1947, and *With Time Running Out* (1950-1956), partly written in Mexico where he went to live in 1952. He still pursued his intensive self-analysis; the poem "A Contemporary" is a disguised self-portrait set in the words of a fictional acquaintance infected by that peevish cynicism into which Cernuda was inclined to fall in moments of bitterness. It is an unflattering portrait, reminiscent of the cold, disdainful image of Cernuda presented by so many critics, but his ability here to see himself as he believed other people saw him argues for a considerable degree of confidence in his own vision of himself. He was, however, deeply troubled at this time by new existential problems as middle age posed a further crisis of identity. He now suffered an internal alienation; when, as in "The Intruder," he looked in the mirror he saw an aging reality that denied the youthful exotic dream he had always carried with him and with which he had continued to identify himself. This problem is partially resolved in the monologue "Yankee Nocturne," which comes to the simple, though unconsoling conclusion, that he is what he is. He could now understand that the erotic ideal was a pretext for self-affirmation and he realized that he could not divorce his present self from what the past had made him. He had therefore to continue to pursue the dream of love that would complete and justify his existence.

In 1949 Cernuda began to take his Summer holidays in Mexico where he finally took up permanent residence in 1952. He found in Mexico an escape from the alien Anglo-Saxon world of exile into a friendly environment that he saw as a transposition of his native Andalusia. The feeling of having regained the lost dream of harmony between self and world, alluded to in the poems "The Traveler" and "Country", was made complete by the love affair Cernuda experienced in Mexico during the summer of 1951, which offered him the possession of that erotic ideal he had created in his youth in Seville. This was the climax of his life, the achievement of the goal for which he had always striven, the fusion of reality and desire. As a sign of this redemption of his youthful dream Cernuda now tended to return to the short song-type poems of his early work in order to condense his experience rather than explore all its possibilities. Also, in the series of love poems "Poems for a Body", included in *With Time Running Out,* he abandoned the objectivizing technique of the second person for a direct first person mode of address as an indication that he had finally found that truth of himself of which he had dreamed in the poem "If a Man Could Only Say" from *Forbidden Pleasures.* "Poems for a Body" reveal the essentially narcissistic concern of the love theme in Cernuda's poetry, although they also show that he was more preoccupied with self-affirmation than with self-love. He now understood that the dream of love was, in fact, a pretext for the search for himself, as the poem "Shadow of Myself" makes clear. The Mexican love affair was that ultimate justification of his existence for which he had always sought, but it was so because through the achievement of his erotic ideal he also achieved his existential ideal.

Cernuda's final collection, *The Disconsolate Chimera* (1956-1962), a title taken from a line in T. S. Eliot's *Four Quartets,* is a poetic last testament. Most of his family, his parents and his two sisters, had died at about the age of sixty, and he feared that he too, who was approaching that age, was soon to die. In the face of this presentiment he was determined in his last poems to set straight his account with life and make a final statement of his beliefs. He was also preoccupied by the unpleasant public image he had acquired, which he regarded as a distortion of the truth he had tried to create in his poems, and he was particularly troubled that this false image would prevail when he was dead. This is the substance of the last poem that he wrote, the *envoi* "To His Countrymen," in which he took a final opportunity to give vent to the acerbic element in his character. The desperate concern to put the record straight causes some of the poems in this last collection to lose the detachment of previous work, although others, like the critique of narcissism in "Ludwig of Bavaria Listens to *Lohengrin,*" are equal to his best poems. The concern, in the face of death, with his public image, is, however, a final indication of the struggle to discover and preserve his personal truth, which is the central motivating force of all Cernuda's poetry.

The presentiment of his imminent death was justified in 1963 when he died of a heart attack in Mexico City. He left behind him in his poems the record of the growth of his character and sensibility through an almost constant condition of stress. But as he struggled to sustain himself, his desire, against the world's hostility he had written the exemplary story of one man's determination to live with dignity and integrity. The resolution with which he pursued his self-analysis, is, in the last resort, more important than his success or failure to find his ideal of harmony between reality and desire. He himself recognized this in the course of a commentary on the work of the 16th-century poet Fray Luis de León: "Fray Luis de León belongs to that class of heroic spirits who are torn between an unattainable ideal and a compelling reality. Such spirits believe that they might attain peace by attaining the possession of their ideal; but we know, and perhaps they also realized it in the depths of their souls, without admitting it, that what gives worth to their lives is not the ideal itself but the dramatic contrast with reality." The clash between reality and desire in Cernuda's own life was the stimulus that led him to seek to come to an understanding of himself through his poetry, and by doing this, so to create himself in his poetry. In an autobiographical essay written in 1958 he declared: "I did not make myself, and I have only tried, like any man, to find *my* truth, which will be neither better nor worse than that of anyone else, just different." Cernuda, in the search for his truth, has provided us with a mirror where we may measure our reflection against his, and recognize in him our own truth, however different that may be.

Derek Harris

Contents

PRIMERAS POESIAS / FIRST POEMS

UN RIO, UN AMOR / A RIVER, A LOVE

LOS PLACERES PROHIBIDOS / FORBIDDEN PLEASURES

DONDE HABITE EL OLVIDO / WHERE OBLIVION DWELLS

INVOCACIONES / INVOCATIONS

LAS NUBES / THE CLOUDS

COMO QUIEN ESPERA EL ALBA /
LIKE SOMEONE WAITING FOR THE DAWN

VIVIR SIN ESTAR VIVIENDO / LIVING WITHOUT BEING ALIVE

CON LAS HORAS CONTADAS / WITH TIME RUNNING OUT

POEMAS PARA UN CUERPO / POEMS FOR A BODY

DESOLACION DE LA QUIMERA / THE DISCONSOLATE CHIMERA

THE POETRY OF LUIS CERNUDA

PRIMERAS POESIAS

Va la brisa reciente
Por el espacio esbelta,
Y en las hojas cantando
Abre una primavera.

Sobre el límpido abismo
Del cielo se divisan,
Como dichas primeras,
Primeras golondrinas.

Tan sólo un árbol turba
La distancia que duerme,
Así el fervor alerta
La indolencia presente.

Verdes están las hojas,
El crepúsculo huye,
Anegándose en sombra
Las fugitivas luces.

En su paz la ventana
Restituye a diario
Las estrellas, el aire
Y el que estaba soñando.

FIRST POEMS

The fresh and tapered
Breeze moves through space
And unfolds a Spring,
Singing in the leaves.

Against the limpid
Abyss of the sky,
Like early joys, first
Swallows greet the eye.

One lone tree disturbs
The sleeping distance,
Thus fervor alerts
Present indolence.

Green are the leaves;
Twilight's escaping;
Drowning in shadow,
The fugitive lights.

At peace, the window
Restores daily
The stars, the air and
He who was dreaming.

Anthony Edkins

Desengaño indolente
Y una calma vacía,
Como flor en la sombra,
El sueño fiel nos brinda.

Los sentidos tan jóvenes
Frente a un mundo se abren
Sin goces ni sonrisas,
Que no amanece nadie.

El afán, entre muros
Debatiéndose aislado,
Sin ayer ni mañana
Yace en un limbo extático.

La almohada no abre
Los espacios risueños;
Dice sólo, voz triste,
Que alientan allá lejos.

El tiempo en las estrellas.
Desterrada la historia.
El cuerpo se adormece
Aguardando su aurora.

Faithful sleep grants us
A languid disillusion
And an empty repose
Like a flower in shadow.

Newly-fledged emotions
Awaken to a world
Without joy or laughter;
No one heralds the day.

Longing, self-absorbed,
Imprisoned by the walls,
Without past or future,
Lies in ecstatic limbo.

The pillow does not lead
To a smiling landscape
But tells, sad-voiced,
How far away it is.

Time belongs to the stars.
The past is banished.
Drowsily, the body
Lies awaiting its dawn.

Derek Harris

Existo, bien lo sé,
Porque le transparenta
El mundo a mis sentidos
Su amorosa presencia.

Mas no quiero estos muros,
Aire infiel a sí mismo,
Ni esas ramas que cantan
En el aire dormido.

Quiero como horizonte
Para mi muda gloria
Tus brazos, que ciñendo
Mi vida la deshojan.

Vivo un solo deseo,
Un afán claro, unánime;
Afán de amor y olvido.
Yo no sé si alguien cae.

Soy memoria de hombre;
Luego, nada. Divinas,
La sombra y la luz siguen
Con la tierra que gira.

I exist, well I know it:
The world to my senses
Clearly reveals
Its amorous presence.

But I don't want these walls,
Air unfaithful to itself,
Or these branches that sing
In air which sleeps.

As a horizon
For my mute glory, I want
Your arms encircling my life
And stripping its petals.

I live one single desire,
One clear unanimous want:
A longing for love and oblivion.
I do not know if someone falls.

I am the memory of a man;
Then, nothing. Divine,
Shadow and light keep going
With the earth which spins.

Anthony Edkins

Los muros nada más.
Yace la vida inerte,
Sin vida, sin ruido,
Sin palabras crueles.

La luz lívida escapa
Y el cristal ya se afirma
Contra la noche incierta,
De arrebatadas lluvias.

Alzada resucita
Tal otra vez la casa;
Los tiempos son idénticos,
Distintas las miradas.

¿He cerrado la puerta?
El olvido me abre
Sus desnudas estancias
Grises, blancas, sin aire.

Pero nadie suspira.
Un llanto entre las manos
Sólo. Silencio; nada.
La oscuridad temblando.

Walls, nothing else.
Lifeless, noiseless,
Without harsh words,
Life lies inert.

Livid light escapes
And glass nerves its glass
Against uncertain night,
With its violent squalls.

Once more as it used to be
The house comes back to life;
Times are just the same,
Different eyes see.

Have I shut the door?
Oblivion opens
Its bare rooms for me,
Grey, white, airless.

But nobody sighs.
My hands have nothing
To hold but tears. Silence;
Darkness trembling; nothing.

Anthony Edkins

Escondido en los muros
Este jardín me brinda
Sus ramas y sus aguas
De secreta delicia.

Qué silencio. ¿Es así
El mundo? Cruza el cielo
Desfilando paisajes,
Risueño hacia lo lejos.

Tierra indolente. En vano
Resplandece el destino.
Junto a las aguas quietas
Sueño y pienso que vivo.

Mas el tiempo ya tasa
El poder de esta hora;
Madura su medida
Escapa entre sus rosas.

Y el aire fresco vuelve
Con la noche cercana,
Su tersura olvidando
Las ramas y las aguas.

Hidden within walls
This garden offers me
The secret delights
Of its branches and water.

How quiet! Is this the way
The world is? Landscapes parade
Beneath the sky
Smiling in the distance.

Languid earth. Fate shines
In vain. By the side
Of still waters, I dream
And think I live.

But time delimits
The sway of this moment;
Its measure ripe,
It escapes among its roses.

And back cool air comes
With the approaching night;
The branches and waters
Forget their tranquility.

Anthony Edkins

UN RIO, UN AMOR

Nevada

En el Estado de Nevada
Los caminos de hierro tienen nombre de pájaro,
Son de nieve los campos
Y de nieve las horas.

Las noches transparentes
Abren luces soñadas
Sobre las aguas o tejados puros
Constelados de fiesta.

Las lágrimas sonríen,
La tristeza es de alas,
Y las alas, sabemos,
Dan amor inconstante.

Los árboles abrazan árboles,
Una canción besa otra canción;
Por los caminos de hierro
Pasa el dolor y la alegría.

Siempre hay nieve dormida
Sobre otra nieve, allá en Nevada.

A RIVER, A LOVE

Nevada

In the State of Nevada
The railroads are named after birds,
The countryside is snow
And time is snow.

The transparent nights
Disclose dream lights on the waters,
Reflect the pure holiday-like
Constellated roof-tops.

Tears smile,
Sadness is winged,
And wings, we know,
Bring fickle love.

Trees embrace trees,
A song kisses another song;
Sadness and happiness
Ride on the railroads.

There is always snow lying asleep on snow
Over there in Nevada.

Anthony Edkins

Como el viento

Como el viento a lo largo de la noche,
Amor en pena o cuerpo solitario,
Toca en vano a los vidrios,
Sollozando abandona las esquinas;

O como a veces marcha en la tormenta,
Gritando locamente,
Con angustia de insomnio,
Mientras gira la lluvia delicada;

Sí, como el viento al que un alba le revela
Su tristeza errabunda por la tierra,
Su tristeza sin llanto,
Su fuga sin objeto;

Como él mismo extranjero,
Como el viento huyo lejos.
Y sin embargo vine como luz.

As the Wind

As the wind throughout the night,
Love in torment or lonely body,
Knocks in vain against the glass,
Abandons corners, sobbing;

Or as at times it runs in the storm,
Insanely shouting,
With anguish of insomnia,
While the delicate rain revolves;

Yes, as the wind by the dawn made to see
Its sorrow wandering over the earth,
Its tearless sorrow,
Its purposeless flight;

As the wind, a foreigner,
As the wind, far away I fly.
And yet, I came as light.

Anthony Edkins

Razon de las lágrimas

La noche por ser triste carece de fronteras.
Su sombra, en rebelión como la espuma,
Rompe los muros débiles
Avergonzados de blancura;
Noche que no puede ser otra cosa sino noche.

Acaso los amantes acuchillan estrellas,
Acaso la aventura apague una tristeza.
Mas tú, noche, impulsada por deseos
Hasta la palidez del agua,
Aguardas siempre en pie quién sabe a cuáles ruiseñores.

Más allá se estremecen los abismos
Poblados de serpientes entre pluma,
Cabecera de enfermos
No mirando otra cosa que la noche
Mientras cierran el aire entre los labios.

La noche, la noche deslumbrante,
Que junto a las esquinas retuerce sus caderas,
Aguardando, quien sabe,
Como yo, como todos.

Reason for Tears

Night being a sad thing lacks frontiers,
Its shadow, rising up like foam,
Shatters weak walls
Overcome with whiteness;
Night which cannot be anything else but night.

Lovers maybe can slash the stars,
Adventure maybe might smother a sadness.
But you, night, pricked on by desires
Towards the pallor of water,
You stand there always waiting for who knows what nightingales.

Farther on are quivering pits
That teem with snakes under every feather;
Pillows for sick men
Who cannot see anything except night
As they still the air between their lips.

Night, dazzling night,
Hugging street-corners, swings her hips,
Waiting for—who knows,
Like me, like us all.

Jack Sage

Dejadme solo

Una verdad es color de ceniza,
Otra verdad es color de planeta;
Mas todas las verdades, desde el suelo hasta el suelo,
No valen la verdad sin color de verdades,
La verdad ignorante de cómo el hombre suele encarnarse
  en la nieve.

En cuanto a la mentira, basta decirle "quiero"
Para que brote entre las piedras
Su flor, que en vez de hojas luce besos,
Espinas en lugar de espinas.

La verdad, la mentira,
Como labios azules,
Una dice, otra dice;
Pero nunca pronuncian verdades o mentiras su secreto torcido;
Verdades o mentiras
Son pájaros que emigran cuando los ojos mueren.

Let Me Alone

One truth has the coloring of ashes,
Another truth has the color of planets;
But all truths, between earth and earth,
Are unworthy of the truth which has no coloring of truths,
The truth which knows nothing of how man becomes incarnate
in the snow.

As for a lie, the words "I love" are all that are needed
For it to burgeon among the stones,
Displaying kisses instead of leaves,
Thorns in place of thorns.

Truth, lies,
Like lips of azure,
Both have their say;
But truth or lies never declare their tortuous secret;
Truth or lies
Are birds that migrate when eyes go dead.

Jack Sage

Carne de mar

Dentro de breves días será otoño en Virginia,
Cuando los cazadores, la mirada de lluvia,
Vuelven a su tierra nativa, el árbol que no olvida,
Corderos de apariencia terrible,
Dentro de breves días será otoño en Virginia.

Sí, los cuerpos estrechamente enlazados,
Los labios en la llave más íntima,
¿Qué dirá él, hecho piel de naufragio
O dolor con la puerta cerrada,
Dolor frente a dolor,
Sin esperar amor tampoco?

El amor viene y va, mira;
El amor viene y va,
Sin dar limosna a nubes mutiladas,
Por vestidos harapos de tierra,
Y él no sabe, nunca sabrá más nada.

Ahora inútil pasar la mano sobre otoño.

Sea Flesh

Within a few days it will be autumn in Virginia,
Hunters, with an expression of rain,
Return to their native land, the tree that doesn't forget,
Lambs of terrifying aspect,
Within a few days it will be autumn in Virginia.

Yes, bodies closely entwined,
Lips on the most intimate key,
What will he say, made a shipwrecked carcase
Or pain with tight-shut door,
Pain facing pain,
But not expecting love either?

Love comes and goes, look;
Love comes and goes,
Gives no alms to crippled clouds,
For clothes, tatters of earth,
And he knows nothing else, and never will.

Useless now to fondle autumn.

Anthony Edkins

LOS PLACERES PROHIBIDOS

Telarañas cuelgan de la razon

Telarañas cuelgan de la razón
En un paisaje de ceniza absorta;
Ha pasado el huracán de amor,
Ya ningún pájaro queda.

Tampoco ninguna hoja,
Todas van lejos, como gotas de agua
De un mar cuando se seca,
Cuando no hay ya lágrimas bastantes,
Porque alguien, cruel como un día de sol en primavera,
Con su sola presencia ha dividido en dos un cuerpo.

Ahora hace falta recoger los trozos de prudencia,
Aunque siempre nos falte alguno;
Recoger la vida vacía
Y caminar esperando que lentamente se llene,
Si es posible, otra vez, como antes,
De sueños desconocidos y deseos invisibles.

Tú nada sabes de ello,
Tú estás allá, cruel como el día;
El día, esa luz que abraza estrechamente un triste muro,
Un muro, ¿no comprendes?,
Un muro frente al cual estoy solo.

FORBIDDEN PLEASURES

Cobwebs Are Hanging from the Mind

Cobwebs are hanging from the mind
In a landscape turned to ash.
The hurricane of love has passed;
No bird remains.

No leaves either;
They have all gone far away,
Like drops of water when a sea dries up,
When there are no longer enough tears,
Because someone, cruel as a sunny day in spring,
Merely by his presence, has cut a body into two.

Now one needs to pick up the pieces prudently,
Although there will always be bits missing,
To lift up one's empty life and journey on
In the hope that, slowly, it will be filled again
As it was before—if that is possible—
With unknown dreams and invisible desires.

You know nothing of that,
You stand aloof, cruel as the day;
Daylight, that light that tightly hugs a sad wall,
—A wall, can't you understand?—
A wall in front of which I stand alone.

Anthony Edkins

No decía palabras

No decía palabras,
Acercaba tan sólo un cuerpo interrogante,
Porque ignoraba que el deseo es una pregunta
Cuya respuesta no existe,
Una hoja cuya rama no existe,
Un mundo cuyo cielo no existe.

La angustia se abre paso entre los huesos,
Remonta por las venas
Hasta abrirse en la piel,
Surtidores de sueño
Hechos carne en interrogación vuelta a las nubes.

Un roce al paso,
Una mirada fugaz entre las sombras,
Bastan para que el cuerpo se abra en dos,
Avido de recibir en sí mismo
Otro cuerpo que sueñe;
Mitad y mitad, sueño y sueño, carne y carne,
Iguales en figura, iguales en amor, iguales en deseo.

Aunque sólo sea una esperanza,
Porque el deseo es una pregunta cuya respuesta nadie sabe.

Said Not a Word

Said not a word,
Just sidled up an inquiring body,
Unaware that desire is a question
Whose answer doesn't exist,
A leaf whose branch doesn't exist,
A world whose heaven doesn't exist.

Agony beats a path through your bones,
Soars through your veins
To burst out over your skin,
Dreamland fountains
Made flesh marked with a question turned cloudwards.

A brief grazing of skins,
A fleeting glance among the shadows,
Are enough to make the body open up,
Avid to take to itself
Another dreaming body:
Half to half, dream to dream, flesh to flesh,
Equal in figure, equal in love, equal in desire.

Even though it's barely a hope,
Because desire is a question whose answer nobody knows.

Jack Sage

Si el hombre pudiera decir

Si el hombre pudiera decir lo que ama,
Si el hombre pudiera levantar su amor por el cielo
Como una nube en la luz;
Si como muros que se derrumban,
Para saludar la verdad erguida en medio,
Pudiera derrumbar su cuerpo, dejando sólo la verdad de su amor,
La verdad de sí mismo,
Que no se llama gloria, fortuna o ambición,
Sino amor o deseo,
Yo sería aquel que imaginaba;
Aquel que con su lengua, sus ojos y sus manos
Proclama ante los hombres la verdad ignorada,
La verdad de su amor verdadero.

Libertad no conozco sino la libertad de estar preso en alguien
Cuyo nombre no puedo oír sin escalofrío;
Alguien por quien me olvido de esta existencia mezquina,
Por quien el día y la noche son para mí lo que quiera,
Y mi cuerpo y espíritu flotan en su cuerpo y espíritu
Como leños perdidos que el mar anega o levanta
Libremente, con la libertad del amor,
La única libertad que me exalta,
La única libertad por que muero.

Tú justificas mi existencia:
Si no te conozco, no he vivido;
Si muero sin conocerte, no muero, porque no he vivido.

If a Man Could Only Say

If a man could only say what he loves,
If a man could raise his love to the heavens
Like a cloud in the light;
If like walls that are demolished
To greet the truth raised behind them
He could demolish his body, leaving only the truth of his love,
The truth of himself,
Which is not called glory, wealth or ambition,
But love or desire,
I would be he who so dreamed;
He who with his tongue, his eyes and his hands
Proclaimed before men the unknown truth,
The truth of his true love.

I know no freedom but the freedom of being confined in someone
Whose name I cannot hear without a shiver;
Someone who makes me forget this wretched existence,
Who makes for me the day and night whatever he wills,
And my body and spirit float in his body and spirit
Like driftwood that the sea lets sink or swim
Freely with the freedom of love,
The only freedom that gives me joy,
The only freedom for which I die.

You justify my existence:
If I do not know you I have not lived;
If I die without knowing you, I do not die, for I have not lived.

Derek Harris

Esperaba solo

Esperaba algo, no sabía qué. Esperaba al anochecer, los sábados. Unos me daban limosna, otros me miraban, otros pasaban de largo sin verme.

Tenía en la mano una flor; no recuerdo qué flor era. Pasó un adolescente que, sin mirar, la rozó con su sombra. Yo tenía la mano tendida.

Al caer, la flor se convirtió en un monte. Detrás se ponía un sol; no recuerdo si era negro.

Mi mano quedó vacía. En su palma apareció una gota de sangre.

I was Waiting Alone

I was waiting for something, I didn't know what. I waited at dusk, on Saturdays. Some gave me alms, others looked at me, still others went by without seeing me.

I had a flower in my hand; I don't remember what flower it was. An adolescent passed; without looking, he grazed it with his shadow. I had my hand stretched out.

The flower fell and turned into a mountain. Behind, a sun was setting. I don't remember if it was black.

My hand was left empty. In its palm a drop of blood appeared.

Anthony Edkins

Como leve sonido

Como leve sonido:
Hoja que roza un vidrio,
Agua que pasa unas guijas,
Lluvia que besa una frente juvenil;

Como rápida caricia:
Pie desnudo sobre el camino,
Dedos que ensayan el primer amor,
Sábanas tibias sobre el cuerpo solitario;

Como fugaz deseo:
Seda brillante en la luz,
Esbelto adolescente entrevisto,
Lágrimas por ser más que un hombre;

Como esta vida no es mía
Y sin embargo es la mía,
Como este afán sin nombre
Que no me pertenece y sin embargo soy yo;

Como todo aquello que de cerca o de lejos
Me roza, me besa, me hiere,
Tu presencia está conmigo fuera y dentro,
Es mi vida misma y no es mi vida,
Así como una hoja y otra hoja
Son la apariencia del viento que las lleva.

Like a Slight Sound

Like a slight sound:
A leaf grazing against glass,
Water passing over pebbles,
Rain kissing a young brow;

Like a quick caress:
A naked foot on the roadway,
Fingers probing first love,
Cool sheets on a lonely body;

Like fleeting desire:
Silk brilliant in the light,
A glimpse of a slender adolescent,
Tears for being more than a man;

Like this life which isn't mine
And yet is mine,
Like this nameless longing
Which doesn't belong to me and yet is me;

Like all that which, from near or far,
Grazes, kisses, wounds me,
Your presence is with me, inside and out,
Is my life itself, and is not my life,
Just as one leaf and another leaf
Define the wind which carries them.

Anthony Edkins

He venido para ver

He venido para ver semblantes
Amables como viejas escobas,
He venido para ver las sombras
Que desde lejos me sonríen.

He venido para ver los muros
En el suelo o en pie indistintamente,
He venido para ver las cosas,
Las cosas soñolientas por aquí.

He venido para ver los mares
Dormidos en cestillo italiano,
He venido para ver las puertas,
El trabajo, los tejados, las virtudes
De color amarillo ya caduco.

He venido para ver la muerte
Y su graciosa red de cazar mariposas,
He venido para esperarte
Con los brazos un tanto en el aire,
He venido no sé por qué;
Un día abrí los ojos: he venido.

Por ello quiero saludar sin insistencia
A tantas cosas más que amables:
Los amigos de color celeste,
Los días de color variable,
La libertad del color de mis ojos:
Los niñitos de seda tan clara,
Los entierros aburridos como piedras,
La seguridad, ese insecto
Que anida en los volantes de la luz.

I've Come to See

I've come to see faces
Dear as old brooms,
I've come to see shadows
Smiling at me from afar.

I've come to see walls
Whether fallen or standing,
I've come to see things,
The sleepy things of these parts.

I've come to see thc seas
Asleep in a little Italian basket,
I've come to see doors,
Work, rooftops, virtues
Of now faded yellow.

I've come to see death
And its funny net for hunting butterflies,
I've come to wait for you,
My arms somewhat in the air,
I've come I don't know why;
One day I opened my eyes: I have come.

Therefore, without insisting, I want to welcome
So many things that are more than pleasant:
Friends of sky-blue color,
Days of variable color,
The freedom of color in my eyes;
Little children in the lightest silk,
Burials as boring as stones,
Security, that insect
Nesting in the folds of light.

Adiós, dulces amantes invisibles,
Siento no haber dormido en vuestros brazos.
Vine por esos besos solamente;
Guardad los labios por si vuelvo.

Goodbye, sweet invisible lovers,
It's sad not to have slept in your arms.
I came only for those kisses;
Look after your lips in case I come back.

Anthony Edkins

DONDE HABITE EL OLVIDO

Donde habite el olvido,
En los vastos jardines sin aurora;
Donde yo sólo sea
Memoria de una piedra sepultada entre ortigas
Sobre la cual el viento escapa a sus insomnios.

Donde mi nombre deje
Al cuerpo que designa en brazos de los siglos,
Donde el deseo no exista.

En esa gran región donde el amor, ángel terrible,
No esconda como acero
En mi pecho su ala,
Sonriendo lleno de gracia aérea mientras crece el tormento.

Allá donde termine este afán que exige un dueño a imagen suya,
Sometiendo a otra vida su vida,
Sin más horizonte que otros ojos frente a frente.

Donde penas y dichas no sean más que nombres,
Cielo y tierra nativos en torno de un recuerdo;
Donde al fin quede libre sin saberlo yo mismo,
Disuelto en niebla, ausencia,
Ausencia leve como carne de niño.

Allá, allá lejos;
Donde habite el olvido.

WHERE OBLIVION DWELLS

Where oblivion dwells,
In vast gardens without a dawn;
Where I shall only be
The memory of a stone, buried among nettles,
Over which the wind escapes its insomnias.

Where my name will leave the body it names
In the arms of the centuries,
Where desire will not exist.

In those great regions where the terrible angel of love
Will not hide his steel-like wing in my breast,
Smiling, full of aerial grace,
While the anguish grows.

There where this longing—which requires a master in its
  own image,
Submitting its life to another life,
No horizon except other eyes, face to face—
There, where this longing will end.

Where sorrow and joy will be only words,
Heaven and earth native to remembrance;
Where, without knowing it, I shall finally be free,
Dispersed in mist, an absence,
Absence, slight as the flesh of a child.

There, there far away;
Where oblivion dwells.

Anthony Edkins

Yo fui.

Columna ardiente, luna de primavera,
Mar dorado, ojos grandes.

Busqué lo que pensaba;
Pensé, como al amanecer en sueño lánguido,
Lo que pinta el deseo en días adolescentes.

Canté, subí,
Fui luz un día
Arrastrado en la llama.

Como un golpe de viento
Que deshace la sombra,
Caí en lo negro,
En el mundo insaciable.

He sido.

I was.

A pillar of fire, spring moon,
Glittering sea, wide eyes.

I searched for what I was thinking;
I thought, as in a languid dream at dawn,
What desire depicts in adolescent days.

I sang, I soared,
Once I was light
Dragged through the flame.

Like a gust of wind
Which destroys shadows,
I fell into blackness,
Into the insatiable world.

I have been.

Anthony Edkins

No es el amor quien muere,
Somos nosotros mismos.

Inocencia primera
Abolida en deseo,
Olvido de sí mismo en otro olvido,
Ramas entrelazadas,
¿Por qué vivir si desaparacéis un día?

Sólo vive quien mira
Siempre ante sí los ojos de su aurora,
Sólo vive quien besa
Aquel cuerpo de ángel que el amor levantara.

Fantasmas de la pena,
A lo lejos, los otros,
Los que ese amor perdieron,
Como un recuerdo en sueños,
Recorriendo las tumbas
Otro vacío estrechan.

Por allá van y gimen,
Muertos en pie, vidas tras de la piedra,
Golpeando impotencia,
Arañando la sombra
Con inútil ternura.

No, no es el amor quien muere.

It is not love that dies
But we ourselves.

Our first innocence
Destroyed in desire,
Oblivion of oneself in another oblivion,
Interlaced branches,
Why live if one day you will disappear?

Only he lives who has
Always before him the eyes of his dawn,
Only he lives who kisses
That angel's body love constructed.

Phantoms of grief,
In the distance, the others,
Those who lost that love,
Like a memory in dreams,
Roaming among the tombs,
They embrace another emptiness.

There they go, moaning,
The living dead, lives beyond the grave,
Beating their impotence,
Clawing at the shadow
With useless tenderness.

No, no, it's not love that dies.

Derek Harris

No hace al muerto la herida,
Hace tan sólo un cuerpo inerte;
Como el hachazo al tronco,
Despojado de sones y caricias,
Todo triste abandono al pie de cualquier senda.

Bien tangible es la muerte;
Mentira, amor, placer no son la muerte.
La mentira no mata,
Aunque su filo clave como puñal alguno;
El amor no envenena,
Aunque como un escorpión deje los besos;
El placer no es naufragio,
Aunque vuelto fantasma ahuyente todo olvido.

Pero tronco y hachazo,
Placer, amor, mentira,
Beso, puñal, naufragio,
A la luz del recuerdo son heridas
De labios siempre ávidos;
Un deseo que no cesa,
Un grito que se pierde
Y clama al mundo sordo su verdad implacable.

Voces al fin ahogados con la voz de la vida.
Por las heridas mismas,
Igual que un río, escapando;
Un triste río cuyo fluir se lleva
Las antiguas caricias,
El antiguo candor, la fe puesta en un cuerpo.

A wound does not make a dead man,
A wound merely leaves him as good as dead,
Like a tree felled by an axe,
Stripped of songs and caresses,
All sad abandonment beside some path.

Death is so very tangible;
Pleasure, love, lies—they are not death.
The lie does not kill,
Although its point, like any dagger, pierces;
Love does not poison,
Although, like a scorpion, it plants its kisses;
Pleasure is not shipwreck,
Although it turns into phantoms that scare oblivion away.

But, in the light of memory,
The trunk of a tree, the blow of an axe,
Pleasure, love, lies,
Kisses, daggers, shipwreck
Are the wounds of always avid lips;
An unceasing desire,
A cry that loses itself
And shouts at the deaf world its implacable truth.

Voices finally choked along with the voice of life.
Through the very same wounds,
Like a river, escaping;
A mournful river whose flow carries with it
Old caresses, old candor,
Faith placed in a body.

No creas nunca, no creas sino en la muerte de todo;
Contempla bien ese tronco que muere,
Hecho el muerto más muerto,
Como tus ojos, como tus deseos, como tu amor;
Ruina y miseria que un día se anegan en inmenso olvido,
Dejando, burla suprema, una fecha vacía,
Huella inútil que la luz deserta.

Believe in nothing, nothing except the death of everything;
Examine closely that tree which is dying
And becoming even more dead than dead,
Like your eyes, like your desires, like your love;
Ruin and misery which will one day sink into immense oblivion,
Leaving behind—the ultimate irony—an empty moment,
A useless footprint deserted by the light.

Anthony Edkins

INVOCACIONES

A las estatuas de los dioses

Hermosas y vencidas soñáis,
Vueltos los ciegos ojos hacia el cielo,
Mirando las remotas edades
De titánicos hombres,
Cuyo amor os daba ligeras guirnaldas
Y la olorosa llama se alzaba
Hacia la luz divina, su hermana celeste.

Reflejo de vuestra verdad, las criaturas
Adictas y libres como el agua iban;
Aún no había mordido la brillante maldad
Sus cuerpos llenos de majestad y gracia.
En vosotros creían y vosotros existíais;
La vida no era un delirio sombrío.

La miseria y la muerte futuras,
No pensadas aún, en vuestras manos
Bajo un inofensivo sueño adormecían
Sus venenosas flores bellas,
Y una y otra vez el mismo amor tornaba
Al pecho de los hombres,
Como ave fiel que vuelve al nido
Cuando el día, entre las altas ramas,
Con apacible risa va entornando los ojos.

Eran tiempos heroicos y frágiles,
Deshechos con vuestro poder como un sueño feliz.
Hoy yacéis, mutiladas y oscuras,
Entre los grises jardines de las ciudades,
Piedra inútil que el soplo celeste no anima,
Abandonadas de la súplica y la humana esperanza.

INVOCATIONS

To the Statues of the Gods

You are dreaming, beautiful and beaten,
Your blind eyes turned towards the heavens,
Regarding the remote ages
Of titanic man;
Their love gave you gentle garlands
And the fragrant flame rose up
Towards the divine light, its celestial sister.

Creatures, devoted and free, moved as water moves,
A reflection of your truth;
Glittering evil had not yet eaten away
Their bodies, full of majesty and grace.
They believed in you and you existed;
Life was not a sombre frenzy.

Misery and death were future things,
Not even thought of; in your hands
Their beautiful poisonous flowers
Were lulled in inoffensive sleep;
And time and again the same love
Returned to the breast of man,
As a faithful bird returns to its nest
Among the high branches when the day,
With gentle laughter, half-closes its eyes.

They were heroic fragile times,
Like a happy dream along with your power undone.
Today you lie, mutilated and obscure,
In gray city gardens, useless stone into which
The celestial breezes no longer breathe life,
And forsaken by prayer and human hope.

La lluvia con la luz resbalan
Sobre tanta muerte memorable,
Mientras desfilan a lo lejos muchedumbres
Que antaño impíamente desertaron
Vuestros marmóreos altares,
Santificados en la memoria del poeta.

Tal vez su fe os devuelva el cielo.
Mas no juzguéis por el rayo, la guerra o la plaga
Una triste humanidad decaída;
Impasibles reinad en el divino espacio.
Distraiga con su gracia el copero solícito
La cólera de vuestro poder que despierta.

En tanto el poeta, en la noche otoñal,
Bajo el blanco embeleso lunático,
Mira las ramas que el verdor abandona
Nevarse de luz beatamente,
Y sueña con vuestro trono de oro
Y vuestra faz cegadora,
Lejos de los hombres,
Allá en la altura impenetrable.

Both rain and sun glide over
So much memorable death
While crowds parade in the distance,
The crowds who, long ago,
Impiously deserted your marble altars,
Consecrated in the poet's memory.

Perhaps the heavens will renew their faith in you.
Don't then judge sorry decadent humanity
With lightning, war or plague;
Reign impassively in divine space.
May the solicitous cup-bearer, with his grace,
Distract the anger of your re-awakened power.

Meanwhile the poet, in the autumn night,
Under the white lunatic ecstasy
Gazes at the branches,
Piously whitening themselves with light
As their greenness abandons them;
He dreams of your golden throne
Of your blinding countenance,
Far away from man,
Out there in the impenetrable heavens.

Anthony Edkins

LAS NUBES

Tristeza del recuerdo

Por las esquinas vagas de los sueños,
Alta la madrugada, fue conmigo
Tu imagen bien amada, como un día
En tiempos idos, cuando Dios lo quiso.

Agua ha pasado por el río abajo,
Hojas verdes perdidas llevó el viento
Desde que nuestras sombras vieron quedas
Su afán borrarse con el sol traspuesto.

Hermosa era aquella llama, breve
Como todo lo hermoso: luz y ocaso.
Vino la noche honda, y sus cenizas
Guardaron el desvelo de los astros.

Tal jugador febril ante una carta,
Un alma solitaria fue la apuesta
Arriesgada y perdida en nuestro encuentro;
El cuerpo entre los hombres quedó en pena.

¿Quién dice que se olvida? No hay olvido.
Mira a través de esta pared de hielo
Ir esa sombra hacia la lejanía
Sin el nimbo radiante del deseo.

Todo tiene su precio. Yo he pagado
El mío por aquella antigua gracia;
Y así despierto, hallando tras mi sueño
Un lecho solo, afuera yerta el alba.

THE CLOUDS

Sadness of Memory

Round the uncertain corners of my dreams,
In the high dawn, your well-loved form went with me
As on a bygone day when God so willed.

Much water has flowed under the bridges;
The wind has carried off its lost green leaves,
Since our two shadows watched unmoved
Their eagerness dissolving as the sun set.

That flame was beautiful, short-lived
Like all that is beautiful: sunlight and sunset.
Deep night came on us, and the ashes kept
The vigil of the stars.

Like a card laid before a feverish gambler,
The wager of a solitary soul
Was hazarded and lost in our encounter;
The body stayed, a phantom among men.

Who says that we forget? There is no forgetting.
Look through this wall of ice, see how that shadow
Goes on toward the distance
Without the radiant nimbus of desire.

Everything has its price. My price was paid
In full for the old favor.
And so I woke, after my dream, to find
A lonely bed, the frozen dawn outside.

Edward M. Wilson

Lázaro

Era de madrugada.
Después de retirada la piedra con trabajo,
Porque no la materia sino el tiempo
Pesaba sobre ella,
Oyeron una voz tranquila
Llamándome, como un amigo llama
Cuando atrás queda alguno
Fatigado de la jornada y cae la sombra.
Hubo un silencio largo.
Así lo cuentan ellos que lo vieron.

Yo no recuerdo sino el frío
Extraño que brotaba
Desde la tierra honda, con angustia
De entresueño, y lento iba
A despertar el pecho,
Donde insistió con unos golpes leves,
Avido de tornarse sangre tibia.
En mi cuerpo dolía
Un dolor vivo o un dolor soñado.

Era otra vez la vida.
Cuando abrí los ojos
Fue el alba pálida quien dijo
La verdad. Porque aquellos
Rostros ávidos, sobre mí estaban mudos,
Mordiendo un sueño vago inferior al milagro,
Como rebaño hosco
Que no a la voz sino a la piedra atiende,
Y el sudor de sus frentes
Oí caer pesado entre la hierba.

Lazarus

It was early morning.
After they had worked hard to lift the stone,
For time, not matter, weighed it down,
They heard a calm voice call me, as a friend
When darkness is falling calls out to another
Who has lagged behind, tired out with travel.
There was a long silence.
This is the story told by those who saw it.

I can remember nothing but strange cold
Sprouting from the deep earth, with agony
Of being half-awake; slowly it moved
—Eager to be transformed to lukewarm blood—
To wake my heart, to urge it with light blows.
My body ached with pain, living or dreamed.

It was life once again.
When I opened my eyes
Pale dawn told me the truth. Because those faces
That eagerly leant over me were dumb
Gnawing the vague dream that fell short of the miracle,
Like the sullen herd
That heeds the herdsman's stone, but not his voice;
And I heard sweat from their foreheads
Heavily falling among the grasses.

Alguien dijo palabras
De nuevo nacimiento.
Mas no hubo allí sangre materna
Ni vientre fecundado
Que crea con dolor nueva vida doliente.
Sólo anchas vendas, lienzos amarillos
Con olor denso, desnudaban
La carne gris y fláccida como fruto pasado;
No el terso cuerpo oscuro, rosa de los deseos,
Sino el cuerpo de un hijo de la muerte.

El cielo rojo abría hacia lo lejos
Tras de olivos y alcores;
El aire estaba en calma.
Mas temblaban los cuerpos,
Como las ramas cuando el viento sopla,
Brotando de la noche con los brazos tendidos
Para ofrecerme su propio afán estéril.
La luz me remordía
Y hundí la frente sobre el polvo
Al sentir la pereza de la muerte.

Quise cerrar los ojos,
Buscar la vasta sombra,
La tiniebla primaria
Que su venero esconde bajo el mundo
Lavando de verguenzas la memoria.
Cuando un alma doliente en mis entrañas
Gritó, por las oscuras galerías
Del cuerpo, agria, desencajada,
Hasta chocar contra el muro de los huesos
Y levantar mareas febriles por la sangre.

Someone spoke of a new birth.
But there was no mother's blood, no fertile womb
With pain creating the new painful life;
Only broad cerements, yellow strips of linen,
Heavy in smell, laid bare
Gray flesh, soft like a sleepy fruit;
Not the smooth dark body, rose of the desires,
But the body of a son of death.

Dawn was breaking, red in the distance
Behind the olive trees and hills;
The air was calm, but the bodies trembled
Like branches in the wind,
Flickered from the dark, stretched out their arms
To offer me their barren toil.
Stung by the light, I buried
My forehead in the dust,
Feeling the lassitude of death.

I tried to close my eyes, to seek
The vast shadow, the primal darkness
That hides its sources underneath the world
And washes memory free of shame.
When an aching soul inside my bowels
Sent through the dark galleries of my body
A bitter, jangling shriek
Until it struck against the wall of bone
And raised the tides of fever in my blood.

Aquel que con su mano sostenía
La lámpara testigo del milagro,
Mató brusco la llama,
Porque ya el día estaba con nosotros.
Una rápida sombra sobrevino.
Entonces, hondos bajo una frente, vi unos ojos
Llenos de compasión, y hallé temblando un alma
Donde mi alma se copiaba inmensa,
Por el amor dueña del mundo.

Vi unos pies que marcaban la linde de la vida,
El borde de una túnica incolora
Plegada, resbalando
Hasta rozar la fosa, como un ala
Cuando a subir tras de la luz incita.
Sentí de nuevo el sueño, la locura
Y el error de estar vivo,
Siendo carne doliente día a día.
Pero él me había llamado
Y en mí no estaba ya sino seguirle.

Por eso, puesto en pie, anduve silencioso,
Aunque todo para mí fuera extraño y vano,
Mientras pensaba: así debieron ellos,
Muerto yo, caminar llevándome a la tierra.
La casa estaba lejos;
Otra vez vi sus muros blancos
Y el ciprés del huerto.
Sobre el terrado había una estrella pálida.
Dentro no hallamos lumbre
En el hogar cubierto de ceniza.

The man who held the lantern,
The witness of the miracle,
Roughly put out the flame,
For the day now was with us.
A fleeting shadow followed.
Then deep below the forehead I saw the eyes
Full of compassion, trembling I found a soul
In which my soul was infinitely copied
By love, mistress of the world.

I saw the feet that marked life's boundary,
The hem of a gray folded tunic
That slipped until it brushed the grave, like a wing
When it prepares to soar into the light.
Again I felt the dream,
The madness and mistake of being alive
When we are flesh that suffers day by day.
But He had called me,
I could do nothing now but follow Him.

And so, once more on foot, I went in silence
Though it was all empty and strange for me,
And I was thinking: "So must they have walked,
So carried me to the earth when I was dead."
The house was far away. Again I saw
Its white walls and the cypress in the garden;
Above the flat roof was a feeble star.
Inside we found no fire
On the ash-covered hearth.

Todos le rodearon en la mesa.
Encontré el pan amargo, sin sabor las frutas,
El agua sin frescor, los cuerpos sin deseo;
La palabra hermandad sonaba falsa,
Y de la imagen del amor quedaban
Sólo recuerdos vagos bajo el viento.
El conocía que todo estaba muerto
En mí, que yo era un muerto
Andando entre los muertos.

Sentado a su derecha me veía
Como aquel que festejan al retorno.
La mano suya descansaba cerca
Y recliné la frente sobre ella
Con asco de mi cuerpo y de mi alma.
Así pedí en silencio, como se pide
A Dios, porque su nombre,
Más vasto que los templos, los mares, las estrellas,
Cabe en el desconsuelo del hombre que está solo,
Fuerza para llevar la vida nuevamente.

Así rogué, con lágrimas,
Fuerza de soportar mi ignorancia resignado,
Trabajando, no por mi vida ni mi espíritu,
Mas por una verdad en aquellos ojos entrevista
Ahora. La hermosura es paciencia,
Sé que el lirio del campo,
Tras de su humilde oscuridad en tantas noches
Con larga espera bajo tierra,
Del tallo verde erguido a la corola alba
Irrumpe un día en gloria triunfante.

All of them gathered round Him at the table.
To me the bread was bitter, the fruit tasteless,
The water tepid, the bodies without desire;
The name of "brother" sounded false
And of love's image there was left
Nothing but vague memories under the wind.
He knew that all was dead in me, that I
Was a dead man, walking among the dead.

Sitting on His right I found myself
Like one who is feasted at his home-coming.
His hand lay near, I leant my head upon it,
Loathing my body and my soul.
So did I pray in silence, as men pray to God,
Because His name, vaster than temples, seas
And stars, can dwell in the affliction of a man
Who is alone—I prayed for
Strength to endure life once more.

So did I ask with tears for
Strength to bear my ignorance with resignation,
To work neither for my life nor for my spirit
But for a truth I had half seen in those eyes
Then. Beauty is patience. I
Know that the lily of the field
After its humble darkness night after night,
Its long waiting under ground, from
Its straight green stalk to its white crown of petals,
Will one day blossom in triumphant glory.

Edward M. Wilson

Impresión de destierro

Fue la pasada primavera,
Hace ahora casi un año,
En un salón del viejo Temple, en Londres,
Con viejos muebles. Las ventanas daban,
Tras edificios viejos, a lo lejos,
Entre la hierba el gris relámpago del río.
Todo era gris y estaba fatigado
Igual que el iris de una perla enferma.

Eran señores viejos, viejas damas,
En los sombreros plumas polvorientas;
Un susurro de voces allá por los rincones,
Junto a mesas con tulipanes amarillos,
Retratos de familia y teteras vacías.
La sombra que caía
Con un olor a gato,
Despertaba ruidos en cocinas.

Un hombre silencioso estaba
Cerca de mí. Veía
La sombra de su largo perfil algunas veces
Asomarse abstraído al borde de la taza,
Con la misma fatiga
Del muerto que volviera
Desde la tumba a una fiesta mundana.

En los labios de alguno,
Allá por los rincones
Donde los viejos juntos susurraban,
Densa como una lágrima cayendo,
Brotó de pronto una palabra: España.
Un cansancio sin nombre
Rodaba en mi cabeza.
Encendieron las luces. Nos marchamos.

Impression of Exile

It was last spring,
Almost a year ago,
In an old drawing-room in the London Temple,
In it old furniture. The window looked out
Past the old buildings into the distance:
Beyond the grass the gray flash of the river.
All was gray, all was weary,
Like the gleam of a sick pearl.

They were old gentlemen, old ladies
With dusty feathers in their hats. There was
A buzz of voices over there in the corner
By tables that supported yellow tulips,
Family photographs and empty tea-pots.
The shadows falling with a smell of cats
Roused noises in the kitchens.

A silent man stood near me. I could see
From time to time his shadowy long profile
Listlessly approach the rim of his tea-cup
With the weariness of a dead man who returns
From the grave to a fashionable party.

From someone's lips, over there in the corner,
Where the old people were murmuring together,
Suddenly, concentrated like a falling tear,
Sprang the one word: "Spain."
Undefinable tiredness
Swirled in my head.
They turned the lights on. We went away.

Tras largas escaleras casi a oscuras
Me hallé luego en la calle,
Y a mi lado, al volverme,
Vi otra vez a aquel hombre silencioso
Que habló indistinto algo
Con acento extranjero,
Un acento de niño en voz envejecida.

Andando me seguía
Como si fuera bajo un peso invisible,
Arrastrando la losa de su tumba;
Mas luego se detuvo.
"¿España?", dijo. "Un nombre.
España ha muerto." Había
Una súbita esquina en la calleja.
Le vi borrarse entre la sombra húmeda.

Down the long stairs almost in darkness,
I came out into the street and, when I turned,
Again I saw the silent man beside me.
He muttered indistinctly something in
A foreign accent.
A boyish accent in an aged voice.

He walked with me
As though he went alone under an invisible weight,
Dragging the slab of his tomb.
Then he stopped.
"Spain?" he said, "A word.
Spain's dead."
There was a sudden crossing in the court,
I saw him blotted out among damp shadows.

Edward M. Wilson

Cementerio en la ciudad

Tras de la reja abierta entre los muros,
La tierra negra sin árboles ni hierba,
Con bancos de madera donde allá a la tarde
Se sientan silenciosos unos viejos.
En torno están las casas cerca hay tiendas,
Calles por las que juegan niños, y los trenes
Pasan al lado de las tumbas. Es un barrio pobre.

Como remiendos de las fachadas grises,
Cuelgan en las ventanas trapos húmedos de lluvia.
Borradas están ya las inscripciones
De las losas con muertos de dos siglos,
Sin amigos que les olviden, muertos
Clandestinos. Mas cuando el sol despierta,
Porque el sol brilla algunos días hacia junio,
En lo hondo algo deben sentir los huesos viejos.

Ni una hoja ni un pájaro. La piedra nada más. La tierra.
¿Es el infierno así? Hay dolor sin olvido,
Con ruido y miseria, frío largo y sin esperanza.
Aquí no existe el sueño silencioso
De la muerte, que todavía la vida
Se agita entre estas tumbas, como una prostituta
Prosigue su negocio bajo la noche inmóvil.

Cuando la sombra cae desde el cielo nublado
Y el humo de las fábricas se aquieta
En polvo gris, vienen de la taberna voces,
Y luego un tren que pasa
Agita largos ecos como bronce iracundo.
No es el juicio aún, muertos anónimos.
Sosegaos, dormid; dormid si es que podéis.
Acaso Dios también se olvida de vosotros.

Urban Cemetery

Behind the railing between walls black earth
—No trees or grass—and wooden benches, where
Old people sit in silence of an evening.
Houses and shops, streets where children play,
Are near it or around it, and the trains
Pass close beside the graves. It is a poor district.

Cloths damp with rain hang from the windows
Like patches on the gray house-fronts.
The epitaphs are obliterated
On the tomb-stones of two centuries of dead
Who have no friends to forget them, the clandestine
Dead. But when the sun wakes
(For the sun shines on a few days about June)
Their old bones must feel something below there.

Not a leaf, not a bird. Stone, nothing else. And earth.
Is Hell like this? Here is grief without forgetfulness
With noise and poverty, long hopeless cold.
Here is no silent sleep of death, for life
Yet moves among these graves, just as a prostitute
Continues business under the still night.

When the shadow falls from the clouded sky
And the factory smoke has dwindled to gray dust,
Shouts come from the public house, a passing train
Shakes the long echoes like an angry bugle.
It is not the Judgment yet; you nameless dead
Keep still and sleep; sleep, if you can sleep.
Perhaps God also has forgotten you.

Edward M. Wilson

Jardin antiguo

Ir de nuevo al jardín cerrado,
Que tras los arcos de la tapia,
Entre magnolios, limoneros,
Guarda el encanto de las aguas.

Oír de nuevo en el silencio,
Vivo de trinos y de hojas,
El susurro tibio del aire
Donde las almas viejas flotan.

Ver otra vez el cielo hondo
A lo lejos, la torre esbelta
Tal flor de luz sobre las palmas:
Las cosas todas siempre bellas.

Sentir otra vez como entonces,
La espina aguda del deseo,
Mientras la juventud pasada
Vuelve. Sueño de un dios sin tiempo.

Old Garden

To go again to the closed garden
Which, behind the wall's open arches
Among magnolias and lemon trees,
Still preserves the charm of water.

To hear again, in the silence
Alive with leaves and the trill of birds,
The cool whisper of the air
Where ancient souls are floating.

To see once more the deep sky
In the distance, the slender tower,
A flower of light above the palms:
All things always fair and handsome.

To feel once more, as then,
The sharp prickle of desire
While past youth returns.
The dream of a god free from time.

Anthony Edkins

La adoración de los Magos

I

Vigilia

Melchor

La soledad. La noche. La terraza.
La luna silenciosa en las columnas.
Junto al vino y las frutas, mi cansancio.
Todo lo cansa el tiempo, hasta la dicha,
Perdido su sabor, después amarga,
Y hoy sólo encuentro en los demás mentira,
Aquí en mi pecho aburrimiento y miedo.
Si la leyenda mágica se hiciera
Realidad algún día.

La profética
Estrella, que naciendo de las sombras
Pura y clara, trazara sobre el cielo,
Tal sobre faz etíope una lágrima,
La estela misteriosa de los dioses.
Ha de encarnarse la verdad divina
Donde oriente esa luz.

¿Será la magia,
Ida la juventud con su deseo,
Posible todavía? Si yo pienso
Aquí, bajo los ojos de la noche,
No es menor maravilla; si yo vivo,
Bien puede un Dios vivir sobre nosotros.
Mas nunca nos consuela un pensamiento,
Sino la gracia muda de las cosas.

The Adoration of the Magi

I

The Eve

Melchior

Solitude. Night. The terrace.
The silent moon amongst the columns.
My weariness beside the fruit and wine.
Time wearies everything, even happiness,
Sapping its taste, turning it bitter,
And today in others I find only deceit,
While within myself boredom and fear.
If only the magic tale would one day
Come true.

Rising pure and clear
From the shadows, the prophetic star
Would trace across the sky,
Like a tear on an Ethiopian cheek,
The mysterious passage of the gods.
Where that star points divine truth
Will be made flesh.

Can the magic
Still be possible when youth and desire
Are past? That I can think here,
Beneath the eyes of the night,
Is no lesser miracle; if I live,
Then a God could well live above us.
But thoughts alone do not console,
Things possessed bring silent grace.

Qué dulce está la noche. Cuando el aire
A la terraza trae desde lejos
Un aroma de nardo y, como un eco,
El són adormecido de las aguas,
Siento animarse en mí la forma vaga
De la edad juvenil con su dulzura.

Así al tiempo sin fondo arroja el hombre
Consuelos ilusorios, penas ciertas,
Y así alienta el deseo. Un cuerpo solo,
Arrullando su miedo y su esperanza,
Desde la sombra pasa hacia la sombra.

Mas tengo sed. Lágrimas de la viña,
Frescas al labio con frescor ardiente,
Tal si un rayo de sol atravesara
La neblina. Delicia de los frutos
De piel tersa y oscura, como un cuerpo
Ofrecido en la rama del deseo.

Señor, danos la paz de los deseos
Satisfechos, de las vidas cumplidas.
Ser tal la flor que nace y luego abierta
Respira en paz, cantando bajo el cielo
Con luz de sol, aunque la muerte exista:
La cima ha de anegarse en la ladera.

Demonio

Gloria a Dios en las alturas del cielo,
Tierra sobre los hombres en su infierno.

How sweet is the night. When the breeze
Brings to the terrace distant perfume
Of spikenard, and, like an echo,
The drowsy murmur of the waters,
I feel the shadowy form of youth,
With all its sweetness, stir within me.

So man throws into bottomless time
His empty joys and certain griefs,
And thus feeds his desire. Just one body,
Soothing his fears and his hopes,
Moves from one shadow into another.

But I am thirsty. Tears of the vine,
Fresh to the lips with burning freshness,
As if a ray of sunlight had pierced
The mist. Sweet taste of fruits
With dark, smooth skins, like a body
Offering itself on the branch of desire.

Lord, grant us the peace of desire
Satisfied, of life fulfilled,
To be as the flower which grows and blooms,
Breathing in peace, singing beneath
The sun-lit sky, even though death exists:
The summit will melt into the slopes.

The Devil

Glory to God in the highest,
Earth over men in their hell.

Melchor

Sin que su abismo lo profane el alba,
Pálida está la noche. Y esa estrella
Más pura que los rayos matinales,
Al dar su luz palpita como sangre
Manando alegremente de la herida.
¡Pronto, Eleazar, aquí!

Hombres que duermen
Y de un sueño de siglos Dios despierta.
Que enciendan las hogueras en los montes,
Llevando el fuego rápido la nueva
A las lindes de reinos tributarios.
Al alba he de partir. Y que la muerte
No me ciegue, mi Dios, sin contemplarte.

II

Los reyes

Baltasar

Como pastores nómadas, cuando hiere la espada del invierno,
Tras una estrella incierta vamos, atravesando de noche
los desiertos,
Acampados de día junto al muro de alguna ciudad muerta,
Donde aúllan chacales; mientras, abandonada nuestra tierra,
Sale su cetro a plaza, para ambiciosos o charlatanes que aún
exploten
El viejo afán humano de atropellar la ley, el orden.
Buscamos la verdad, aunque verdades en abstracto son cosa
innecesaria,
Lujo de soñadores, cuando bastan menudas verdades acordadas.
Mala cosa es tener el corazón henchido hasta dar voces, clamar
por la verdad, por la justicia.
No se hizo el profeta para el mundo, sino el dúctil sofista
Que toma el mundo como va: guerras, esclavitudes, cárceles y
verdugos
Son cosas naturales, y la verdad es sueño, menos que sueño, humo.

Melchior

Though dawn does not defile its void,
The night grows pale. And that star,
Purer than the sun's rays at morning,
Throbs as it sheds its light, flowing
Joyously like blood from a wound.
Here, Eleazar, at once!

While men sleep
God awakens from an age-long slumber.
Let the signal fires be lit on the hills,
The flames will quickly take the news
To the far frontiers of my lands.
I shall leave at dawn. And may death
Not blind me, my God, until I see you.

II

The Kings

Balthasar

Like nomad shepherds, when winter's sword is unsheathed,
We wander after a star, crossing the deserts at night,
Camping by day beneath the walls of some dead city
Where jackals howl; while in the lands we left behind
Our sceptres are bid for by grasping scoundrels
Who still exploit man's old desire to overthrow law and order.
We seek the truth, although men do not need abstract truths,
That luxury of dreamers, when ordinary, little truths suffice.
It is not good for the heart to swell up, crying out for truth
and justice.
The prophet was not made for this world, but the pliant sophist
Who takes the world as he finds it: wars, slavery, prisons and
executioners
Are natural things, and the truth is a dream, less than a dream, a
wisp of smoke.

Gaspar

Amo el jardín, cuando abren las flores serenas del otoño,
El rumor de los árboles, cuya cima dora la luz toda reposo,
Mientras por la avenida el agua esbelta baila sobre el mármol
Y a lo lejos se escucha, entre el aire más denso, un pájaro.
Cuando la noche llega, y desde el río un viento frío corre
Sobre la piel desnuda, llama la casa al hombre,
Hecha voz tibia, entreabiertos sus muros como una concha oscura,
Con la perla del fuego, donde sueño y deseo juntan sus luces
puras.
Un cuerpo virgen junto al lecho aguarda desnudo, temeroso,
Los brazos del amante, cuando a la madrugada penetra y duele
el gozo.
Esto es la vida. ¿Qué importan la verdad o el poder junto a esto?
Vivo estoy. Dejadme así pasar el tiempo en embeleso.

Melchor

No hay poder sino en Dios, en Dios sólo perdura la delicia;
El mar fuerte es su brazo, la luz alegre su sonrisa.
Dejad que el ambicioso con sus torres oscurezca la tierra;
Pasto serán del huracán, con polvo y sombra confundiéndolas.
Dejad que el lujurioso bese y muerda, espasmo tras espasmo;
Allá en lo hondo siente la indiferencia virgen de los huesos
castrados.
¿Por qué os doléis, oh reyes, del poder y la dicha que atrás
quedan?
Aunque mi vida es vieja no vive en el pasado, sino espera;
Espera los momentos más dulces, cuando el alma regale
La gracia, y el cuerpo sea al fin risueño, hermoso e ignorante.
Abandonad el oro y los perfumes, que el oro pesa y los aromas
aniquilan.
Adonde brilla desnuda la verdad nada se necesita.

Baltasar

Antífona elocuente, retórica profética de raza a quien escapa con
el poder la vida.
Pero mi pueblo es joven, es fuerte, y diferente del tuyo israelita.

Gaspar

I love the garden, when the gentle flowers of Autumn open,
The rustling of the trees, whose tops glow in the peaceful light,
While along the avenue graceful water dances on marble
And in the distance a bird sings in the darkening air.
When night comes and from the river a cool breeze flows
Over naked flesh, man's home calls to him,
Like a soothing voice, its walls half-open as in a dark shell,
With the fire for a pearl, where dream and desire are fused in pure light.
A virgin body waits naked and timorous beside the bed
For the lover's arms, before dawn when pleasure penetrates and pains.
This is life. What good are truth or power beside this?
I am alive. Let me pass away the time in rapture.

Melchior

There is no power but in God, in God alone does delight endure;
The strong sea is his arm, the joyful light his smile.
Let the ambitious man cover the land with his towers;
They will be garnered by the hurricane, turned to dust and shadow.
Let the lascivious man kiss and bite, spasm after spasm;
Deep within himself he feels the virgin apathy of castrated bones.
Why do you grieve, oh Kings, for the power and happiness you left behind?
Although my life is old, it lives not in the past, but hopes;
Hopes for the sweetest moments when grace will clothe the soul,
And the body will be at last full of joy, innocence and beauty.
Let be gold and perfumes, for gold is heavy and perfumes fade.
Where truth shines naked nothing more is needed.

Balthasar

Psalmaic eloquence, prophetic rhetoric of a race whom power and life desert.
But my people are young and strong, different from you Israelites.

Gaspar

Si el beso y si la rosa codicio, indiferente hacia los dioses todos,
Es porque beso y rosa pasan. Son más dulces los efímeros gozos.

Melchor

Locos enamorados de las sombras ¿olvidáis, tributarios
Como son vuestros reinos del mío, que aún puedo sujetaros
A seguir entre siervos descalzos el rumbo de mi estrella?
¿Qué es soberbia o lujuria ante el miedo, el gran pecado, la fuerza de la tierra?

Baltasar

Con tu verdad pudiera, si la hallamos, alzar un gran imperio.

Gaspar

Tal vez esa verdad, como una primavera, abra rojos deseos.

III

Palinodia de la esperanza divina

Era aquel que cruzábamos, camino
Abandonado entre arenales,
Con una higuera seca, un pozo, y el asilo
De una choza desierta bajo el frío.
Lejos, subiendo entre unos riscos,
Iba el pastor junto a sus flacas cabras negras.
Cuando tras de la noche larga la luz vino,
Irisando la escarcha sobre nuestros vestidos,
Faltas de convicción las cosas escaparon
Como en un sueño interrumpido.

Gaspar

If I long for a kiss and a rose, indifferent to all gods,
It is because kiss and rose fade. Fleeting pleasures are sweetest.

Melchior

Madmen enamoured of shadows, do you forget that your kingdoms
Are subject to me, that I can still force you to follow
The track of my star, among the barefoot slaves?
What is pride or pleasure beside the fear, the great sin, the force of the earth?

Balthasar

With your truth, if we find it, we might raise a great empire.

Gaspar

Perhaps, like the Spring, that truth will unveil crimson desires.

III

Palinode of Divine Hope

That path we travelled
Led us through a sandy waste,
With a dry fig-tree, a well, and the shelter
Of an abandoned hut in the cold.
Far off, climbing amongst the crags,
Was a shepherd with his scrawny black goats.
When the light came after the long night,
Making the frost on our clothes glisten,
Things seemed unreal and vanished,
As in a dream disturbed.

Padecíamos hambre, gran fatiga.
Al lado de la choza hallamos una viña
Donde un racimo quedaba todavía,
Seco, que ni los pájaros lo habían
Querido. Nosotros lo tomamos:
De polvo y agrio vino el paladar teñía,
Era bueno el descanso, pero
En quietud la indiferencia del paisaje aísla,
Y añoramos la marcha, la fiebre de la ida.

Vimos la estrella hacia lo alto
Que estaba inmóvil, pálida como el agua
En la irrupción del día, una respuesta dando
Con su brillo tardío del milagro
Sobre la choza. Los muros sin cobijo
Y el dintel roto se abrían hacia el campo,
Desvalidos. Nuestro fervor helado
Se volvió como el viento de aquel páramo.
Dimos el alto. Todos descabalgaron.
Al entrar en la choza, refugiados
Una mujer y un viejo sólo hallamos.

Pero alguien más había en la cabaña:
Un niño entre sus brazos la mujer guardaba.
Esperamos un dios, una presencia
Radiante e imperiosa, cuya vista es la gracia,
Y cuya privación idéntica a la noche
Del amante celoso sin la amada.
Hallamos una vida como la nuestra humana,
Gritando lastimosa, con ojos que miraban
Dolientes, bajo el peso de su alma
Sometida al destino de las almas,
Cosecha que la muerte ha de segarla.

We suffered hunger and great weariness.
Beside the hut we found a vine
Where still a bunch of grapes remained,
So dry not even the birds had
Wanted it. We took it:
Staining our mouths with its dust and bitter wine.
It was good to rest, but the silence
In the empty land made us feel alone,
We missed the fever of the journey, the need to go on.

High up in the sky we saw
That the star, as pale as water at daybreak,
Had stopped over the hut, as though to echo
The miracle with its tardy gleam.
The tumble-down walls and gaping doorway
Gave no shelter, standing open
To the land outside. Our eagerness
Turned cold as the wind in that desert.
We came to a halt. Everyone dismounted.
When we went into the hut we found only
A woman and an old man taking refuge there.

But someone else was there in the hut:
The woman held a child in her arms.
We had hoped for a god, a shining,
Commanding presence, whom to see is grace
And from whom to be separated is like the night
Of a jealous lover parted from his beloved.
We found a life like our human life,
Crying pitifully, with eyes gazing out in grief,
Beneath the burden of its soul,
Subject to the destiny of all souls,
A harvest for death to reap.

Nuestros dones, aromas delicados y metales puros,
Dejamos sobre el polvo, tal si la ofrenda rica
Pudiera hacer al dios. Pero ninguno
De nosotros su fe viva mantuvo,
Y la verdad buscada sin valor quedó toda,
El mundo pobre fue, enfermo, oscuro.
Añoramos nuestra corte pomposa, las luchas y las guerras,
O las salas templadas, los baños, la sedosa
Carne propicia de cuerpos aún no adultos,
O el reposo del tiempo en el jardín nocturno,
Y quisimos ser hombres sin adorar a dios alguno.

IV

Sobre el tiempo pasado

Mira cómo la luz amarilla de la tarde
Se tiende con abrazo largo sobre la tierra
De la ladera, dorando el gris de los olivos
Otoñales, ya henchidos por los frutos maduros;

Mira allá las marismas de niebla luminosa.
Aquí, año tras año, nuestra vida transcurre,
Llevando los rebaños de día por el llano,
Junto al herboso cauce del agua enfebrecida;

De noche hacia el abrigo del redil y la choza.
Nunca vienen los hombres por estas soledades,
Y apenas si una vez les vemos en el zoco
Del mercado vecino, cuando abre la semana.

Esta paz es bien dulce. Callada va la alondra
Al gozar de sus alas entre los aires claros.
Mas la paz, que a las cosas en ocio santifica,
Aviva para el hombre cosecha de recuerdos.

In the dust we left our gifts, delicate perfumes
And pure metals, as if a rich offering
Could make him a god. But not one
Of us kept his faith alive.
And the truth we had sought lost its meaning,
The world was poor, dark and infirm.
We longed for the pomp of our courts, struggles and wars,
Or cool chambers, baths, the silken flesh
Found only in adolescent bodies,
Or the haven from time in the garden at night,
And we wanted to be men with no gods to worship.

IV

On Time Past

Look how the yellow light of evening
Spreads its long embrace over the earth
On the hillside, gilding the autumn-gray
Of olives heavy now with ripe fruit.

Look there at the mist shining on the swamp.
Here, year after year, our life goes by,
By day we take the flocks across the plain
Beside the brackish water's grassy banks;

At night we shelter in fold and hut.
Men never come to these lonely places
And rarely do we see them in the town,
In the market, at the week's beginning.

This peace is sweet. The lark wings silent
To enjoy its flight in the clear air.
But peace, which sanctifies useless things,
Awakens in man a host of memories.

Tiempo atrás, siendo joven, divisé una mañana
Cruzar por la llanura un extraño cortejo:
Jinetes en camellos, cubiertos de ropajes
Cenicientos, que daban un destello de oro.

Venían de los montes, pasados los desiertos,
De los reinos que lindan con el mar y las nieves,
Por eso era su marcha cansada sobre el polvo
Y en sus ojos dormía una pregunta triste.

Eran reyes que el ocio y el poder enloquecieron,
En la noche siguiendo el rumbo de una estrella,
Heraldo de otro reino más rico que los suyos.
Pero vieron la estrella pararse en este llano,

Sobre la choza vieja, albergue de pastores.
Entonces fue refugio dulce entre los caminos
De una mujer y un hombre sin hogar ni dineros:
Un hijo blanco y débil les dio la madrugada.

El grito de las bestias acampando en el llano
Resonó con las voces en extraños idiomas,
Y al entrar en la choza descubrieron los reyes
La miseria del hombre, de que antes no sabían.

Luego, como quien huye, el regreso emprendieron.
También los caminantes pasaron a otras tierras
Con su niño en los brazos. Nada supe de ellos.
Soles y lunas hubo. Joven fui. Viejo soy.

Gentes en el mercado hablaron de los reyes:
Uno muerto al regreso, de su tierra distante;
Otro, perdido el trono, esclavo fue, o mendigo;
Otro a solas viviendo, presa de la tristeza.

Long ago, when I was young, I saw a strange
Caravan cross the plain one morning.
Men on camels, wearing dusty clothes
That gave off a glimmer of gold.

They came from the hills, beyond the desert,
From lands that border on the sea and snow,
This was why they moved so slowly in the dust
And a sad question slept in their eyes.

They were kings made mad by power and leisure,
Following through the night the track of a star
That heralded another kingdom richer than theirs.
But they saw the star stop on this plain,

Over an old hut, a shepherds' cabin.
Then it was sweet shelter on the road
For a man and woman without home or money:
The dawn gave them a weak, pale child.

The cries of the animals tethered on the plain
Mingled with voices in foreign tongues,
And the Kings found, inside the hut,
Man's poverty, which before they had not known.

Then, as though in flight, they set off back.
The travelers also went to other lands
With their child in their arms. I heard nothing of them.
Suns and moons passed. I was young. I am old.

People in the market spoke of the Kings:
One died on the journey, far from his land;
Another lost his throne, made beggar or slave;
Another lived alone, a prey to sadness.

Buscaban un dios nuevo, y dicen que le hallaron.
Yo apenas vi a los hombres; jamás he visto dioses.
¿Cómo ha de ver los dioses un pastor ignorante?
Mira el sol desangrado que se pone a lo lejos.

V

Epitafio

La delicia, el poder, el pensamiento
Aquí descansan. Ya la fiebre es ida.
Buscaron la verdad, pero al hallarla
  No creyeron en ella.

Ahora la muerte acuna sus deseos,
Saciándolos al fin. No compadezcas
Su sino, más feliz que el de los dioses
  Sempiternos, arriba.

They sought a new god, and some say they found him.
I rarely saw men. I have never seen any gods.
How can an ignorant shepherd see gods?
Look over there at the blood-red setting sun.

V

Epitaph

Delight, power, thought, find here
Repose. The fever is past.
They sought the truth, and found it,
        But did not believe.

Now death lulls their desires,
Sated at last. Pity not
Their fate, less harsh than that of
        Deathless gods above.

Derek Harris

Gaviotas en los parques

Dueña de los talleres, las fábricas, los bares
Toda piedras oscuras bajo un cielo sombrío,
Silenciosa a la noche, los domingos devota,
Es la ciudad levítica que niega sus pecados.

El verde turbio de la hierba y los árboles
Interrumpe con parques los edificios uniformes,
Y en la naturaleza sin encanto, entre la lluvia,
Mira de pronto, penacho de locura, las gaviotas.

¿Por qué, teniendo alas, son huéspedes del humo,
El sucio arroyo, los puentes de madera de estos parques?
Un viento de infortunio o una mano inconsciente,
De los puertos nativos, tierra adentro las trajo.

Lejos quedó su nido de los mares, mecido por tormentas
De invierno, en calma luminosa los veranos.
Ahora su queja va, como el grito de almas en destierro.
Quien con alas las hizo, el espacio les niega.

Gulls in the Parks

Mistress of workshops, factories and bars,
Mass of dark stones under a heavy sky,
Silent at night, devout on Sundays, this
Is the pharisaical city that disowns its sins.

The muddy green of grass and trees in parks
Breaks in on regimented buildings, and
In the disenchanted scenery and rain
Suddenly, look—a tuft of folly—the gulls.

Winged, why are they lodgers in the smoke,
Dirty streams, wooden bridges of these parks?
Winds of misfortune or unknowing hands
Bore them up-country from their native ports.

Far behind lie their nests at sea, rocked
By winter storms, or in sunlit calm of summer.
Now their complaint is like the cry of exiled
Souls. God gave them wings, denies them space.

Edward M. Wilson

COMO QUIEN ESPERA EL ALBA

Las ruinas

Silencio y soledad nutren la hierba
Creciendo oscura y fuerte entre ruinas,
Mientras la golondrina con grito enajenado
Va por el aire vasto, y bajo el viento
Las hojas en las ramas tiemblan vagas
Como al roce de cuerpos invisibles.

Puro, de plata nebulosa, ya levanta
El agudo creciente de la luna
Vertiendo por el campo paz amiga,
Y en esta luz incierta las ruinas de mármol
Son construcciones bellas, musicales,
Que el sueño completó.

Esto es el hombre. Mira
La avenida de tumbas y cipreses, y las calles
Llevando al corazón de la gran plaza
Abierta a un horizonte de colinas:
Todo está igual, aunque una sombra sea
De lo que fue hace siglos, mas sin gente.

Levanta ese titánico acueducto
Arcos rotos y secos por el valle agreste
Adonde el mirto crece con la anémona,
En tanto el agua libre entre los juncos
Pasa con la enigmática elocuencia
De su hermosura que venció a la muerte.

LIKE SOMEONE WAITING FOR THE DAWN

The Ruins

Silence and solitude nourish the grass
That grows dark and strong amongst the ruins,
While swallows wheel through the boundless air
With anguished cries, and beneath the wind
The leaves on the trees tremble softly
As if brushed by invisible bodies.

The sharp crescent of the waxing moon
Rises, pure and misty-silvered,
Shedding its friendly peace over the land,
And in this uncertain light the marble ruins
Are a beautiful, musical edifice
Made whole by a dream.

Such is man. Look at
The avenue of cypresses and tombs,
The streets leading to the heart of the great square
Lying open to a horizon of hills:
Nothing has changed, even though it is a shadow
Of itself centuries ago, but the people have gone.

That titanic aqueduct's dry broken arches
Stride across the untilled valley
Where the myrtle grows beside the anemone,
While the water flows free among the reeds
With the enigmatic eloquence
Of beauty that has conquered death.

En las tumbas vacías, las urnas sin cenizas,
Conmemoran aún relieves delicados
Muertos que ya no son sino la inmensa muerte anónima,
Aunque sus prendas leves sobrevivan:
Pomos ya sin perfume, sortijas y joyeles
O el talismán irónico de un sexo poderoso,
Que el trágico desdén del tiempo perdonara.

Las piedras que los pies vivos rozaron
En centurias atrás, aún permanecen
Quietas en su lugar, y las columnas
En la plaza, testigos de las luchas políticas,
Y los altares donde sacrificaron y esperaron,
Y los muros que el placer de los cuerpos recataban.

Tan sólo ellos no están. Este silencio
Parece que aguardase la vuelta de sus vidas.
Mas los hombres, hechos de esa materia fragmentaria
Con que se nutre el tiempo, aunque sean
Aptos para crear lo que resiste al tiempo,
Ellos en cuya mente lo eterno se concibe,
Como en el fruto el hueso encierran muerte.

Oh Dios. Tú que nos has hecho
Para morir, ¿por qué nos infundiste
La sed de eternidad, que hace al poeta?
¿Puedes dejar así, siglo tras siglo,
Caer como vilanos que deshace un soplo
Los hijos de la luz en la tiniebla avara?

Mas tú no existes. Eres tan sólo el nombre
Que da el hombre a su miedo y su impotencia,
Y la vida sin ti es esto que parecen
Estas mismas ruinas bellas en su abandono:
Delirio de la luz ya sereno a la noche,
Delirio acaso hermoso cuando es corto y es leve.

On the empty tombs, the urns without ashes,
Delicate reliefs still commemorate
The dead who now are only immense anonymous death,
Although their trifling possessions still survive:
Pomanders now without perfume, rings and jewels,
Or the ironic talisman of a once powerful sex,
Which the tragic disdain of time has spared.

The stones that living feet trod
Centuries ago, remain still motionless
In their place, and the columns in the square
That witnessed the politicians' struggles,
And the altars where they sacrificed and hoped,
And the walls that veiled the pleasures of the flesh.

Only the people are not here. This silence
Seems to await the return of their lives.
But men, made of that fragmentary material
With which time is nourished, even though
They can create things that stand against time,
They in whose mind eternity is conceived,
Have within them, like a fruit's stone, death.

Oh God. You who have made us to die,
Why did you fill us with the thirst
For eternity that creates the poet?
Can you allow the sons of light to fall,
Century after century, into the greedy shadow
Like thistle-down blown away on the wind?

But you do not exist. You are only the name
Man gives to his fear and impotence,
And life without you is like
These splendid ruins here in desolation:
A frenzy of light calmed by the dusk,
A frenzy almost beautiful when it is brief and mild.

Todo lo que es hermoso tiene su instante, y pasa.
Importa como eterno gozar de nuestro instante.
Yo no te envidio, Dios; déjame a solas
Con mis obras humanas que no duran:
El afán de llenar lo que es efímero
De eternidad, vale tu omnipotencia.

Esto es el hombre. Aprende pues, y cesa
De perseguir eternos dioses sordos
Que tu plegaria nutre y tu olvido aniquila.
Tu vida, lo mismo que la flor, ¿es menos bella acaso
Porque crezca y se abra en brazos de la muerte?

Sagrada y misteriosa cae la noche,
Dulce como una mano amiga que acaricia,
Y en su pecho, donde tal ahora yo, otros un día
Descansaron la frente, me reclino
A contemplar sereno el campo y las ruinas.

All things beautiful have their moment, and vanish.
We must grasp our moment as if it were eternal.
I do not envy you, God; leave me alone
With my human works that do not endure:
The desire to fill what is ephemeral
With eternity is equal to your omnipotence.

Such is man. Learn then, and stop pursuing
Deaf, eternal gods nourished by your prayer
And destroyed when you forget them.
Is your life any less beautiful because
It grows and blooms, like the flower, in death's embrace?

The night falls sacred and mysterious,
Sweet as the caress of a friendly hand,
And in the breast where once others
Laid their brow, I now lie back
To gaze in peace at the landscape and the ruins.

Derek Harris

Juventud

¿Es más bella la hoja
Verde, que su deseo?
¿Luz estival de oro,
O nimbo de embeleso?

Mejor que la palabra,
El silencio en que duerme.
No la pasión: el sueño
Adonde está latente.

Al ser irreductible,
La nube primitiva
Prefiere; las futuras
Criaturas divinas.

Esa indecisa gracia
Tan pura de la fuente,
No el mar; y esa sonrisa
Que al amor antecede.

No el arco triunfante
De meta conseguida:
La inicial misteriosa
Y eterna de la vida.

Youth

Is the green leaf
More beautiful than its desire?
Golden summer rays—
Or an aureole of delight?

Rather than the spoken word,
The silence that cradles it.
Not passion—the dream
Wherein it is latent.

Instead of irreducible being,
Choose the pristine cloud,
The divine creatures
Yet to be found.

That wavering grace
Of the fountain, untouched—
Not the sea; and that smile
Which precedes love.

Not the triumphal arch
Of the goal won by strife—
The initiation, mysterious
And eternal, of life.

Jack Sage

La familia

¿Recuerdas tú, recuerdas aún la escena
A que día tras día asististe paciente
En la niñez, remota como sueño al alba?
El silencio pesado, las cortinas caídas,
El círculo de luz sobre el mantel, solemne
Como paño de altar, y alrededor sentado
Aquel concilio familiar, que tantos ya cantaron,
Bien que tú, de entraña dura, aún no lo has hecho.

Era a la cabecera el padre adusto,
La madre caprichosa estaba en frente,
Con la hermana mayor imposible y desdichada,
Y la menor más dulce, quizá no más dichosa,
El hogar contigo mismo componiendo,
La casa familiar, el nido de los hombres,
Inconsistente y rígido, tal vidrio
Que todos quiebran, pero nadie dobla.

Presidían mudos, graves, la penumbra,
Ojos que no miraban los ojos de los otros,
Mientras sus manos pálidas alzaban como hostia
Un pedazo de pan, un fruto, una copa con agua,
Y aunque entonces vivían en ellos presentiste,
Tras la carne vestida, el doliente fantasma
Que al rezo de los otros nunca calma
La amargura de haber vivido inútilmente.

Suya no fue la culpa si te hicieron
En un rato de olvido indiferente,
Repitiendo tan sólo un gesto trasmitido
Por otros y copiado sin una urgencia propia,
Cuya intención y alcance no pensaban.
Tampoco fue tu culpa si no les comprendiste:
Al menos has tenido la fuerza de ser franco
Para con ellos y contigo mismo.

The Family

Do you remember, remember still that scene
Where you sat patiently day after day
In your childhood, remote now like a dream at dawn?
The heavy silence, the drawn curtains,
The circle of light around the dining-table,
As solemn as an altar, where there sat
That family conclave, praised by so many before,
Although you, less tender-hearted, have not yet done so.

At the head sat your stern, stiff father,
Facing him was your impractical mother,
With your elder sister, ill-fated and disabled,
And the younger one, more gentle, but perhaps no less fortunate;
They, who with you, comprised the family,
The hearth and home, that human nest,
Fragile and unyielding, like glass,
Which anyone can break, but none can bend.

In the shadow, expressionless, unsmiling eyes
Watched, avoiding the gaze of other eyes,
While their pallid hands raised, like the host,
A piece of bread, a fruit, a glass of water,
And even then, while they lived, you felt in them,
Behind the clothed flesh, that anguished phantom,
Which, despite others' prayers, can never still
The bitterness of having lived in vain.

It was not their fault if they made you
In a moment of unthinking forgetfulness,
They were only repeating an action, passed on by
Others and copied without any personal need,
To whose purpose and import they gave no thought.
Neither was it your fault if you did not understand them;
You have, at least, had the strength to be honest
With them and with yourself.

Se propusieron, como los hombres todos, lo durable,
Lo que les aprovecha, aunque en torno miren
Que nada dura en ellos ni aprovecha,
Que nada es suyo, ni ese trago de agua
Refrescando sus fauces en verano,
Ni la llama que templa sus manos en invierno,
Ni el cuerpo que penetran con deseo
Dos soledades en una carne sola.

Ellos te dieron todo: cuando animal inerme
Te atendieron con leche y con abrigo;
Después, cuando creció tu cuerpo a par del alma,
Con dios y con moral te proveyeron,
Recibiendo deleite tras de azuzarte a veces
Para tu fuerza tierna doblegar a sus leyes.
Te dieron todo, sí: vida que no pedías,
Y con ella la muerte de dura compañera.

Pero algo más había, agazapado
Dentro de ti, como alimaña en cueva oscura,
Que no te dieron ellos, y eso eres:
Fuerza de soledad, en ti pensarte vivo,
Ganando tu verdad con tus errores.
Así, tan libremente, el agua brota y corre,
Sin servidumbre de mover batanes,
Irreductible al mar, que es su destino.

Aquel amor de ellos te apresaba
Como prenda medida para otros,
Y aquella generosidad, que comprar pretendía
Tu asentimiento a cuanto
No era según el alma tuya.
A odiar entonces aprendiste el amor que no sabe
Arder anónimo sin recompensa alguna.

They sought, like all men, to create something lasting,
Something of benefit, although around them they saw
That nothing of theirs lasts or benefits them,
That nothing belongs to them, not even that glass of water
With which they refresh their throats in summer,
Nor the flame warming their hands in winter,
Nor the body they enter with desire,
Two solitudes made one single flesh.

They gave you everything; as a defenseless animal,
They cared for you with milk and warmth;
Later, when your body grew in step with your soul,
They supplied you with a god and a morality,
Taking pleasure sometimes after chastising you
So that your tender strength might bend to their laws.
They gave you everything, yes, a life you did not want,
And with it death, as a cruel companion.

But there was something else, huddled
Inside you, like a beast in its dark lair,
Which they did not give you, and this is what you are:
Strength of my solitude, I shall live in you,
Finding your truth through your mistakes,
Just as water springs and runs free,
Untrammelled by the need to turn machines,
Unchanging down to the sea, which is its destiny.

That love of theirs held you fast,
Like a garment made for someone else,
And that generosity, which sought
To buy your consent to anything
That did not accord with your nature.
You learnt then to hate that love which does not know
How to burn unknown without reward.

El tiempo que pasó, desvaneciéndolos
Como burbuja sobre la haz del agua,
Rompió la pobre tiranía que levantaron,
Y libre al fin quedaste, a solas con tu vida,
Entre tantos de aquellos que, sin hogar ni gente,
Dueños en vida son del ancho olvido.
Luego con embeleso probando cuanto era
Costumbre suya prohibir en otros
Y a cuyo trasgresor la excomunión seguía,
Te acordaste de ellos, sonriendo apenado.
Cómo se engaña el hombre y cuán en vano
Da reglas que prohiben y condenan.
¿Es toda acción humana, como estimas ahora,
Fruto de imitación y de inconsciencia?

Por esta extraña llama hoy trémula en tus manos,
Que aun deseándolo, temes ha de apagarse un día.
Hasta ti transmitida con la herencia humana
De experiencias inútiles y empresas inestables
Obrando el bien y el mal sin proponérselo,
No prevalezcan las puertas del infierno
Sobre vosotros ni vuestras obras de la carne,
Oh padre taciturno que no le conociste,
Oh madre melancólica que no le comprendiste.

Que a esas sombras remotas no perturbe
En los limbos finales de la nada
Tu memoria como un remordimiento.
Este cónclave fantasmal que los evoca,
Ofreciendo tu sangre tal bebida propicia
Para hacer a los idos visibles un momento,
Perdón y paz os traiga a ti y a ellos.

The time that has passed, obliterating them
Like a bubble on the water's surface,
Broke the wretched tyranny they had created,
And you were left free at last, alone with your life,
Among so many who, without home or people,
Are the masters in life of boundless oblivion.
Then, tasting enraptured all that it was
Their custom to prohibit in others,
With excommunication for those who disobey,
You remembered them, with a pained smile.
How man deceives himself and how futile
Are the rules he makes to prohibit and condemn.
Are all the acts of man, as you now believe,
The fruit of imitation and unconsciousness?

For this strange flame still trembling in your hands,
Which, while wanting it, you fear will one day die,
Passed on to you with that human inheritance
Of useless experience and fragile enterprise,
Doing good and evil without meaning to,
For the sake of this flame may the gates of hell
Not prevail over you nor the products of your flesh,
Silent father, who never came to know your son,
Sad mother, who never understood him.

May those distant shades be not disturbed
In the uttermost limbo of the void
By their memory of you, like a pang of remorse.
May this ghostly gathering that invokes them,
Offering your blood like a libation
To make the departed visible for a moment,
Bring peace and pardon to you and to them.

Derek Harris

Primavera vieja

Ahora, al poniente morado de la tarde,
En flor ya los magnolios mojados de rocío,
Pasar aquellas calles, mientras crece
La luna por el aire, será soñar despierto.

El cielo con su queja harán más vasto
Bandos de golondrinas; el agua en una fuente
Librará puramente la honda voz de la tierra;
Luego el cielo y la tierra quedarán silenciosos.

En el rincón de algún compás, a solas
Con la frente en la mano, un fantasma
Que vuelve, llorarías pensando
Cuán bella fue la vida y cuán inútil.

Spring Long Ago

Now, in the purple west of the evening,
Flowering magnolias, wet with dew,
To walk along those streets now, while the moon
Grows in the sky, will be to dream awake.

Flocks of swallows will make the sky vaster
With their protest; water in a fountain
Will release the pure deep voice of the earth;
And then, both sky and earth will stay silent.

In the corner of some secluded place, alone,
Hand on your brow, like a returning ghost,
You would be sitting, tears in your eyes, thinking
How beautiful life was, and how useless.

Anthony Edkins

Los espinos

Verdor nuevo los espinos
Tienen ya por la colina,
Toda de púrpura y nieve
En el aire estremecida.

Cuántos ciclos florecidos
Les has visto; aunque a la cita
Ellos serán siempre fieles,
Tú no lo serás un día.

Antes que la sombra caiga,
Aprende cómo es la dicha
Ante los espinos blancos
Y rojos en flor. Vé. Mira.

The Hawthorns

The hawthorns on the hill
Have already fresh attire,
All purple and snow
In the shivering air.

How many flowering cycles
Have you seen; though they'll always be
Faithful at the appointed hour,
You, one day, will not be.

Before the shadow falls,
Learn about happiness
From red and white hawthorns
In flower. Look. See.

Anthony Edkins

Noche del hombre y su demonio

D: Vive la madrugada. Cobra tu señorío.
Percibe la existencia en dolor puro.
Ahora el alma es oscura, y los ojos no hallan
Sino tiniebla en torno. Es ésta la hora cierta
Para hablar de la vida, la vida tan amada.
Si al Dios de quien es obra le reprochas
Que te la diera limitada en muerte,
Su don en sueños no malgastes. Hombre, despierta.

H: Entre los brazos de mi sueño estaba
Aprendiendo a morir. ¿Por qué me acuerdas?
¿Te inspira acaso envidia el sueño humano?
Amo más que la vida este sosiego a solas,
Y tú me arrancas de él, para volverme
Al carnaval de sombras, por el cual te deslizas
Con ademán profético y paso insinuante
Tal ministro en desgracia. No quiero verte. Déjame.

D: No sólo forja el hombre a imagen propia
Su Dios, aún más se le asemeja su demonio.
Acaso mi apariencia no concierte
Con mi poder latente: aprendo hipocresía,
Envejezco además, y ya desmaya el tiempo
El huracán sulfúreo de las alas
En el cuerpo del ángel que fui un día.
En mí tienes espejo. Hoy no puedo volverte
La juventud huraña que de ti ha desertado.

A Man's Night with His Demon

Demon: Wake to the small hours. Regain your dominion.
Look on existence as undiluted pain.
Now the soul is dark and the eyes find nothing
About them but shadow. This is the right time
To speak of life, of your beloved life.
If you reproach the God whose work it is,
Because he gave it you curbed by death,
Do not waste his gift in dreams. Man, awake.

Man: In the arms of sleep I was learning
To die. Why do you rouse me from it?
Are you perhaps jealous of man's sleep?
I love this solitary peace more than
Life itself, and you drag me away,
Back to the carnival of shadows
Where you move with ominous and unctuous
Bearing, like a minister in disgrace.
I do not want to see you. Let me be.

Demon: Man not only makes his God in his own
Image, his demon bears an even closer
Likeness to him. Perhaps my appearance
Is out of keeping with my hidden power:
I learn to dissemble, and, what's more, grow old;
And time already weakens the brimstone
Tempest in the wings of the angel's body
That once I was. In me you see yourself.
Today I cannot bring back the timid
Days of youth that have deserted you.

H: En la hora feliz del hombre, cuando olvida,
Aguzas mi conciencia, mi tormento;
Como enjambre irritado los recuerdos atraes;
Con sarcasmo mundano suspendes todo acto,
Dejándolo incompleto, nulo para la historia,
Y luego, comparando cuánto valen
Ante un chopo con sol en primavera
Los sueños del poeta, susurras cómo el sueño
Es de esta realidad la sombra inútil.

D: Tu inteligencia se abre entre el engaño:
Es como flor a un viejo regalada,
Y a poco que la muerte se demore,
Ella será clarividente un día.
Mas si el tiempo destruye la sustancia,
Que aquilate la esencia ya no importa.
Ha sido la palabra tu enemigo:
Por ella de estar vivo te olvidaste.

H: Hoy me reprochas el culto a la palabra.
¿Quién si no tú puso en mí esa locura?
El amargo placer de transformar el gesto
En són, sustituyendo el verbo al acto,
Ha sido afán constante de mi vida.
Y mi voz no escuchada, o apenas escuchada,
Ha de sonar aún cuando yo muera,
Sola, como el viento en los juncos sobre el agua.

D: Nadie escucha una voz, tú bien lo sabes.
¿Quién escuchó jamás la voz ajena
Si es pura y está sola? El histrión elocuente,
El hierofante vano miran crecer el corro
Propricio a la mentira. Ellos viven, prosperan;
Tú vegetas sin nadie. El mañana ¿qué importa?
Cuando a ellos les olvide el destino, y te recuerde,
Un nombre tú serás, un són, un aire.

Man: In man's happy moments, when he forgets,
You sharpen my awareness, my torment;
You bring an angry swarm of memories;
You forestall each act with blasé sarcasm,
Leaving it unfinished, a void in time,
And then, comparing the poet's dreams
To the worth of a poplar in the spring sun
You whisper to me that the dream is
This reality's futile shadow.

Demon: Your mind opens to its delusion,
Like a flower given to an old man,
And if death does not come too soon,
You will, one day, see this all too clear.
But if time destroys the substance,
That it enhance the essence is pointless.
It is words that have been your enemy:
For their sake you forgot to be alive.

Man: Today you chide me for my creed of words.
Who but you set that madness in me?
The bitter pleasure of turning action
Into sound, replacing deed with word,
Has been the constant struggle of my life.
And my unheeded, or barely heeded
Voice, shall sound even when I am dead,
Alone, like the wind among the rushes.

Demon: No one heeds a voice, as well you know.
Whoever listened to another's voice,
When pure and alone? The glib buffoon
And vapid hierophant see their lies greeted
By crowds' acclaim. They live, they prosper;
You languish alone. Who cares for tomorrow?
When fate forgets them and remembers you
As just a name, a sound, a breath of air.

H: Me hieres en el centro más profundo,
Pues conoces que el hombre no tolera
Estar vivo sin más: como en un juego trágico
Necesita apostar su vida en algo,
Algo de que alza un ídolo, aunque con barro sea,
Y antes que confesar su engaño quiere muerte.
Mi engaño era inocente, y a nadie arruinaba
Excepto a mí, aunque a veces yo mismo lo veía.

D: Siento esta noche nostalgia de otras vidas.
Quisiera ser el hombre común de alma letárgica
Que extrae de la moneda beneficio,
Deja semilla en la mujer legítima,
Sumisión cosechando con la prole,
Por pública opinión ordena su conciencia
Y espera en Dios, pues frecuentó su templo.

H: ¿Por qué de mí haces burla duramente?
Si pierde su sabor la sal del mundo
Nada podrá volvérselo, y tú no existirías
Si yo fuese otro hombre más feliz acaso,
Bien que no es la cuestión el ser dichoso.
Amo el sabor amargo y puro de la vida,
Este sentir por otros la conciencia
Aletargada en ellos, con su remordimiento,
Y aceptar los pecados que ellos mismos rechazan.

D: Pobre asceta irrisorio, confiesa cuánto halago
Ofrecen el poder y la fortuna:
Alas para cernerse al sol, negar la zona
En sombra de la vida, gratificar deseos,
Con dúctil amistad verse fortalecido,
Comprarlo todo, ya que todo está en venta,
Y contemplando la miseria extraña
Hacer más delicado el placer propio.

Man: You strike at my being's very center,
Since you know man cannot tolerate life
Without support; as in some tragic game
He must wager his life on something,
Something he makes an idol, even though of clay,
And would die rather than admit his pretense.
My pretense was guileless, and hurt no one
But myself, although I knew this at times.

Demon: Tonight I pine for a different life,
To be a common man with leaden soul
Who uses money to make money,
Leaves his seed in his lawful wedded wife,
Rewarded by submissive off-spring,
Obedient to public opinion,
And hoping in God, since he goes to church.

Man: Why do you mock me so cruelly?
If the world loses its attraction,
It goes for ever, and you would not exist
Were I another, perhaps happier man,
Although happiness is irrelevant.
I love the pure, bitter taste of life,
Assuming for others the conscience
Made supine in them, and their remorse,
Accepting the sins which they reject.

Demon: Poor foolish ascetic, admit how much
Delight lies in power and fortune,
Wings to fly in the sun-light, to deny
Life's shadows, to gratify desires,
To see yourself sustained by fawning friends,
To buy anything, since all is for sale,
And by observing others' poverty
To make your own pleasure more exquisite.

H: Dos veces no se nace, amigo. Vivo al gusto
De Dios. ¿Quién evadió jamás a su destino?
El mío fue explorar esta extraña comarca,
Contigo siempre a zaga, subrayando
Con tu sarcasmo mi dolor. Ahora silencio,
Por si alguno pretende que me quejo: es más digno
Sentirse vivo en medio de la angustia
Que ignorar con los grandes de este mundo,
Cerrados en su limbo tras las puertas de oro.

D: Después de todo, ¿quién dice que no sea
Tu Dios, no tu demonio, el que te habla?
Amigo ya no tienes sino es éste
Que te incita y despierta, padeciendo contigo.
Mas mira cómo el alba a la ventana
Te convoca a vivir sin ganas otro día.
Pues el mundo no aprueba al desdichado,
Recuerda la sonrisa y, como aquel que aguarda,
Alzate y vé, aunque aquí nada esperes.

Man: We are not born twice my friend. I live
As God wills. Who can escape his fate?
Mine was to explore these strange marches
With you always behind me, heightening
My pain with your sarcasm. Now be quiet,
In case someone thinks I am complaining.
It is better to live amidst anguish
Than to dwell in ignorance like the world's
Great men, stagnating behind golden doors.

Demon: After all, who is to say this isn't your God,
And not your demon, who is speaking to you?
You no longer have a friend but this one
Who arouses you, suffering with you.
But look how the dawn at the window
Calls you to live unwillingly another day.
Since the world disapproves of misfortune,
Bring back your smile, stand up, look about you
In hope, though you can expect nothing here.

Derek Harris

VIVIR SIN ESTAR VIVIENDO

El intruso

Como si equivocara el tiempo
   Su trama de los días
¿Vives acaso los de otro?,
   Extrañas ya la vida.

Lejos de ti, de la conciencia
   Desacordada, el centro
Buscas afuera, entre las cosas
   Presentes un momento.

Así de aquel amigo joven
   Que fuiste ayer, aguardas
En vano ante el umbral de un sueño
   La ilusa confianza.

Pero tu faz, en el alinde
   De algún espejo, vieja,
Hosca, abstraída, te interrumpe
   Tal la presencia ajena.

Hoy este intruso eres tú mismo,
   Tú, como el otro antes,
Y con el cual sin gusto inicias
   Costumbre a que se allane.

Para llegar al que no eres,
   Quien no eres te guía,
Cuando el amigo es el extraño
   Y la rosa es la espina.

LIVING WITHOUT BEING ALIVE

The Intruder

As if time had confused
    The thread of its days,
Are you by chance living out somebody else's?
    Life is a stranger to you.

Far from yourself, from your consciousness
    In disarray, you search
For the center out there among things
    Momentarily present.

And so, on the threshold of a dream
    In vain you wait
For the illusive trust of that young friend
    Who was you yesterday.

But your face, reflected
    By some distorting mirror, old,
Sullen, far removed, breaks in
    As an alien presence.

Today that intruder is yourself,
    Where before it was that somebody else;
Joylessly you now start to get them
    Used to each other.

In order to reach the one who is not you,
    The one you are not guides you,
While friend is stranger,
    And the rose is the thorn.

Jack Sage

Un Contemporáneo

Le conocí hace ya tanto tiempo;
Déjeme que recuerde. Si la memoria falla
A mi edad, cuando trata de imaginarse algo
Que en años mozos fuimos, aún más cuando persigue
La figura del hombre sólo visto un momento.

Nunca pensé que alguien viniera a preguntarme
Por tal persona, sin familiar, amigo,
Posición o fortuna; viviendo oscuramente,
Con los gestos diarios de cualquiera
A quien ya nadie nombra tras de muerto.

Que de espejo nos sirva
El prójimo, y nuestra propia imagen
Observemos en él, mas no la suya,
Ocurre a veces. Quien interroga a otros
Por un desconocido, debe contentarse
Con lo que halla, aun cuando sea huella
Ajena superpuesta a la que busca.

Era de edad mediana
Al conocerlo yo, enseñando,
No sé, idioma o metafísica, en puesto subalterno,
Como extraño que ha de ganar la vida
Por malas circunstancias y carece de apoyo.

A esta ciudad había venido
Desde el norte donde antes estuvo
En circunstancias aún peores; ya conoce
Aquella gente práctica y tacaña, que buscando
Va por la vida sólo rendimiento,
Y poco rendimiento de tal hombre traslucía.

A Contemporary

I met him such a long time ago now;
Let me try to remember. If memory fails me
At my age, when it seeks to imagine something
We were in our years of youth, it is even weaker
When seeking the face of a man seen only for a moment.

I never thought that anyone would come to ask me
About such a person, without family, friends,
Position or fortune, living in obscurity
With the commonplace bearing of any man
Who will never be mentioned after his death.

It sometimes happens that our neighbor
Is a mirror for ourselves and we see in him
Our own image and not his. Anyone who asks
Another about a stranger must be content
With what he finds, even when it is an alien
Profile superimposed on the one he seeks.

He was middle-aged
When I met him, teaching,
I don't know, languages or metaphysics, in a junior
Position, like an outsider who must earn his living
In unpleasant circumstances and without help.

He had come to this city from the north
Where he had been before
In still worse circumstances; he was already acquainted
With that practical, mean race whose
Only purpose in life is to profit from others,
And little profit was to be had in such a man.

Aquí se hallaba a gusto, en lo posible
Para quien no parecía a gusto en parte alguna,
Aun cuando, ido, no quisiera
Regresar, ni a varios conocidos
Locales recordó. Así trataba acaso
Que lo pasado fuera pasado realmente
Y comenzar en limpio nueva etapa.

No le vi mucho, rehusando,
A lo que entiendo, el trato y compañía,
Acasa huraño y receloso en algo
Para mí indiferente. Poco hablaba,
Aunque en rara ocasión hablaba todo
Lo callado hasta entonces, entero, abrupto,
Y pareciendo luego avergonzado.

Pero seamos francos: yo no le quería
Bien, y un día, conversando
Temas insustanciales, el tiempo, los deportes,
La política, sentí temor extraño
Que en burla, no hacia mí, sino a los hombres todos
En mí representados, fuera a sacar la lengua.

Lo que pensó, amó, odió, le dejó indiferente,
Ignoro; como lo ignoro igual hasta de otros
Que conocí mejor. Nuestro vivir, de muchedumbre
A solas con un dios, un demonio o una nada,
Supongo que era el suyo también. ¿Por qué no habría de serlo?

Su pensamiento hoy puede leerse
Tras la obra, y ella sabrá decirle
Más que yo. Aunque supongo
Tales escritos sin valor alguno,
Y aquí ninguno se cuidaba de su autor o ellos.

Here he was at ease, as far as was possible
For someone who seemed never at ease anywhere;
Although when he left, he did not wish
To return, nor remembered the several
People he had known here. Perhaps he tried like this
To make the past really past
And so begin a new, unsullied period in his life.

I didn't see him often, from what I understand
He avoided people and social contact.
Perhaps he was shy and distrustful about something
I had no interest in. He said little,
Although on rare occasions he would say
All he had suppressed until then, completely, brusquely,
And then seemed to be ashamed by it.

But let's be frank: I didn't really like him,
And one day, chatting about trivial things,
The weather, sport, politics, I felt
A strange fear that he was going to mock
Not me, but all men represented by me.

What he thought, loved, hated, felt indifferent to,
I do not know, as I do not know about others
With whom I am more acquainted. Our life,
In a crowd alone with god, devil, or nothing,
Was, I suppose, his as well. Why shouldn't it be?

His thoughts can today be read
In his works, and these will tell you more about him
Than I can. Although I don't suppose
Those writings are of any value.
And here no one cared about them or their author.

Esta fama postrera no la mueve,
En mozos tan despiertos, amor de hacer justicia,
Sino gusto de hallar razón contra nosotros
Los viejos, el estorbo palmario en el camino,
Al cual no basta el apartar, mas el desprecio
Debe añadirse. Pues, ¿acaso
Vive desconocido el poeta futuro?

Sabemos que un poeta es otra cosa;
La chispa que le anima pronto prende
En quienes junto a él cruzan la vida,
Sus versos aceptados tal moneda corriente.
Lope fue siempre el listo Lope, vivo o muerto.

Tan vulgar como quiera será el vulgo,
Pero la voz del vulgo es voz divina,
Por estos tiempos nuestros a lo menos;
Y el vulgo era ignorante de ese hombre
Mientras viviera, en signo
Que siempre ignorará su póstuma excelencia.

La sociedad es justa, a todos trata
Como merecen; si hay exceso
Primero, con idéntico exceso retrocede,
Recobrando nivel. Piense de alguno,
Festejado tal dios por muchedumbres,
Por esas muchedumbres tal animal colgado.
Bien que ello nos repugne, justicia pura y simple.

This latterday fame is not the result
Of a love of justice in such aware young men,
But caused by a wish to find something against us,
The old ones, who stand in the way of their success,
And who must not only be pushed aside,
But despised as well. Is it possible, then,
For a future poet to live unknown?

We know that a poet is something different.
The spark that burns within him quickly catches
Those who cross his path in life,
His verses are accepted like legal tender.
Lope always was the brilliant Lope, alive or dead.*

However common people may become,
The voice of the people is a divine voice,
At least in these times of ours.
And people were ignorant of that man
While he lived, as a sign
That they would always ignore his worth after his death.

Society is just, it treats everyone according to
His merits; if at first there is excess,
With the same excess it withdraws, regaining
Equilibrium. Think of those,
Fêted like gods by the crowd,
Then hung like an animal by that same crowd.
Although it repels us, this is justice pure and simple.

* *Lope:* Lope de Vega (1562-1635), one of the foremost playwrights of the Spanish classical theatre who achieved immense popularity during his lifetime.

Mas eso no se aplica a nuestro hombre.
¿Acaso hubo exceso en el olvido
Que vivió día a día? Hecho a medida
Del propio ser oscuro, exacto era; y a la muerte
Se lleva aquello que tomamos
De la vida, o lo que ella nos da: olvido
Acá, y olvido allá para él. Es lo mismo.

But this does not apply to our man.
Was there perhaps excess in the oblivion
He lived through day after day? It was made
To measure exactly for his own obscure being.
And in death we take with us what we took
From life or what it gave us: oblivion
Here and oblivion there; it's all the same.

Derek Harris

Cara joven

Ahora quisieras recordarte,
Hablar lo mismo que solías
Antes, de ligero y de breve,
Por amor a esta faz tan niña.

Pero los tiempos ya son otros,
Y tú otro del que creías
Entonces. Sólo tu gozo
Es el de siempre si la miras.

Como lluvia clara, conforta;
Como sueño de amanecida,
Alienta; sugiere posibles
E imposibles, como la vida.

Young Face

You'd like to remember yourself,
To speak, with brevity and ease,
The same now as formerly,
All for love of this young face.

But times are other than they were
And you are other than the one
You thought you were then. Only your delight,
When looking at it, is the same.

Like clear rain, it brings comfort;
Like a dream at dawn, it inspires;
It suggests things possible
And impossible, just like life.

Anthony Edkins

CON LAS HORAS CONTADAS

Nocturno yanqui

La lámpara y la cortina
Al pueblo en su sombra excluyen.
Sueña ahora,
Si puedes, si te contentas
Con sueños, cuando te faltan
Realidades.

Estás aquí, de regreso
Del mundo, ayer vivo, hoy
Cuerpo en pena,
Esperando locamente,
Alrededor tuyo, amigos
Y sus voces.

Callas y escuchas. No. Nada
Oyes, excepto tu sangre,
Su latido
Incansable, temoroso;
Y atención prestas a otra
Cosa inquieta.

Es la madera, que cruje;
Es el radiador, que silba.
Un bostezo.
Pausa. Y el reloj consultas:
Todavía temprano para
Acostarte.

WITH TIME RUNNING OUT

Yankee Nocturne

The lamp-light and drawn curtain
Shut out the darkened town.
Dream now,
If you can, if you are content
With dreams, when you lack
Realities.

Here you are, back from the world,
Yesterday alive, today a body
In torment,
Hoping frantically for
Friends and their voices
Around you.

You keep quiet and listen.
No. Nothing to hear but the pulse
Of your blood,
Untiring and fearful;
Then you notice another
Distraction.

It's the wood, creaking;
It's the radiator, hissing;
A yawn.
A pause. And you look at your watch:
It is still too early for you
To go to bed.

Tomas un libro. Mas piensas
Que has leído demasiado
Con los ojos,
Y a tus años la lectura
Mejor es recuerdo de unos
Libros viejos,
Pero con nuevo sentido.

¿Qué hacer? Porque tiempo hay.
Es temprano.
Todo el invierno te espera,
Y la primavera entonces.
Tiempo tienes.

¿Mucho? ¿Cuánto? ¿Y hasta cuándo
El tiempo al hombre le dura?
"No, que es tarde,
Es tarde," repite alguno
Dentro de ti, que no eres.
Y suspiras.

La vida en tiempo se vive,
Tu eternidad es ahora,
Porque luego
No habrá tiempo para nada
Tuyo. Gana tiempo. ¿Y cuándo?

Alguien dijo:
"El tiempo y yo para otros
Dos." ¿Cuáles dos? ¿Dos lectores
De mañana?
Mas tus lectores, si nacen,
Y tu tiempo, no coinciden.
Estás solo
Frente al tiempo, con tu vida
Sin vivir.

You pick up a book. But you think
That you have read too much
With your eyes,
And old books read before
Are better at your age,
Remembered
With a new meaning.

What to do? Because there's time.
It's early.
All the Winter awaits you
And afterwards the Spring.
You have time.

Much time? How much? And until when
Does time hold out for man?
"No, it's late,
It's late," repeats someone
Inside you, who is not you.
And you sigh.

Life is lived in time.
Your eternity is now,
Because later
There will be no time for anything
Of yours. Make time. But when?

Someone said:
"Time and myself for two other
People." Which two? Two readers
In the future?
But your readers, if there are any,
And your time, do not tally.
You are alone
Facing time, with your life
Unlived.

Remordimiento.
Fuiste joven,
Pero nunca lo supiste
Hasta hoy, que el ave ha huido
De tu mano.

La mocedad dentro duele,
Tú su presa vengadora,
Conociendo
Que, pues no le va esta cara
Ni el pelo blanco, es inútil
Por tardía.

El trabajo alivia a otros
De lo que no tiene cura,
Según dicen.
¿Cuántos años ahora tienes
De trabajo? ¿Veinte y pico
Mal contados?

Trabajo fue que no compra
Para ti la independencia
Relativa.
A otro menester el mundo,
Generoso como siempre,
Te demanda.

Y profesas pues, ganando
Tu vida, no con esfuerzo,
Con fastidio.
Nadie enseña lo que importa,
Que eso ha de aprenderlo el hombre
Por sí solo.

A pang of remorse.
You were young,
But you never knew it until
Today when the bird has flown
From your hand.

Your youth aches within you,
Taking its revenge on you,
Because it knows
That with this mis-matched face
And gray hair, it is too late
To be of use.

Work brings comfort to others
For things that have no cure,
So they say.
How many years now have you
Been working? Twenty odd,
Maybe more?

It was work that has not brought
For you any real measure
Of freedom.
The world, generous as always,
Demands of you some other
Occupation.

And so you teach, earning
Your living, without effort but
With disgust.
No one can teach what matters,
A man has to learn that
On his own.

Lo mejor que has sido, diste,
Lo mejor de tu existencia,
A una sombra:
Al afán de hacerte digno,
Al deseo de excederte,
Esperando
Siempre mañana otro día
Que, aunque tarde, justifique
Tu pretexto.

Cierto que tú te esforzaste
Por sino y amor de una
Criatura,
Mito moceril, buscando
Desde siempre, y al servirla,
Ser quien eres.

Y al que eras le has hallado.
¿Mas es la verdad del hombre
Para él solo,
Como un inútil secreto?
¿Por qué no poner la vida
A otra cosa?

Quien eres, tu vida era;
Uno sin otro no sois,
Tú lo sabes.
Y es fuerza seguir, entonces,
Aun el miraje perdido,
Hasta el día
Que la historia se termine,
Para ti al menos.

The best that you have been,
The best of your life, you gave
To a shadow:
To the longing to redeem yourself,
To the desire to transcend yourself,
Always waiting
For another day tomorrow
Which, though late, would justify
Your pretense.

True, it was your destiny
To strive for the love of a
Human being,
A youthful myth, always sought,
And by serving it to be
Who you are.

And you have found who you were.
But is a man's truth
For him alone,
Like a useless secret?
Why not put your life to
Some other use?

You are now what your life was;
You are not one without the other,
You know that.
And you must carry on then,
Still after the lost mirage,
Until the day
When the story comes to an end,
For you at least.

Y piensas
Que así vuelves
Donde estabas al comienzo
Del soliloquio: contigo
Y sin nadie.

Mata la luz, y a la cama.

And so you think
That you are back
Where you were at the start
Of your soliloquy: alone
With yourself.

Put out the light and go to bed.

Derek Harris

Versos para ti mismo

La noche y el camino. Mientras,
La cabeza recostada en tu hombro,
El cabello suave a flor de tu mejilla,
Su cuerpo duerme o sueña acaso.

No. Eres tú quien sueña solo
Aquel efecto noble compartido,
Cuyos ecos despiertan por tu mente desierta
Como en la concha los del mar que ya no existe.

Verses for Yourself

Night and the road. Meanwhile,
Head reclining on your shoulder,
Soft hair stroking your cheek,
His body sleeps, dreams perhaps.

No. It's you alone who dreams
That noble shared effect;
In your deserted mind its echoes stir
As in a shell those of the sea which is no longer there.

Anthony Edkins

El viajero

Eres tú quien respira
Este cálido aire
Nocturno, entre las hojas
Perennes. ¿No te extraña

Ir así, en el halago
De otro clima? Parece
Maravilla imposible
Estar tan libre. Mira

Desde una palma oscura
Gotear las estrellas.
Lo que ves ¿es tu sueño
O tu verdad? El mundo

Mágico que llevabas
Dentro de ti, esperando
Tan largamente, afuera
Surge a la luz. Si ahora

Tu sueño al fin coincide
Con tu verdad, no pienses
Que esta verdad es frágil,
Más aún que aquel sueño.

The Traveler

It's you who's breathing
This warm night air
Among the evergreen leaves.
Doesn't it surprise you,

Getting along like this
In another climate's arms?
It seems an impossible
Marvel to be so free.

Look, stars are cascading
From a black palm tree.
Is what you see your dream
Or your truth? The magic

World you carried inside you,
Waiting for so long a time,
Is emerging towards
The light outside. If now

At last your dream coincides
With your truth, try to forget
This truth's fragile, even
More fragile than that dream.

Anthony Edkins

Pais

Tus ojos son de donde
La nieve no ha manchado
La luz y entre las palmas
El aire
Invisible es de claro.

Tu deseo es de donde
A los cuerpos se alía
Lo animal con la gracia
Secreta
De mirada y sonrisa.

Tu existir es de donde
Percibe el pensamiento,
Por la arena de mares
Amigos,
La eternidad en tiempo.

Country

Your eyes are from where
The snow has not stained
The light and among the palms
The air's so bright
It is invisible.

Your desire is from where
The secret animal grace
Of glance and smile
Is allied
With bodies.

Your existence is from where
Thought perceives,
By the sand of friendly
Seas,
Eternity in time.

Anthony Edkins

Amor en musica

Aunque el tema sea el mismo,
Cada amor tiene su aire,
Que con tantas variaciones
Difiere y a nuevo sabe.

La primavera en los ojos
Lleva uno, y el verano
El otro en la piel, o al menos
Eso cree el enamorado.

Pero en todos el infierno
Está oculto, hasta el instante
De las lágrimas, del grito
Que de las entrañas sale.

Pues luego al infierno llevan,
Por eso a veces quisiste
Evitar sus paraísos
Con una prudencia triste.

Pero, amigo ¿y a la música
Quién se niega, si es dotado
De oído bueno, ni al deseo
Ojos buenos que ven claro?

Si éstos nacen para locos
Y aquéllos para prudentes,
De qué lado estás ya sabes:
Canta tus aires fielmente.

Y deja la melodía
Llenarte todo el espíritu
Ya qué más da gozo o pena
Si en el amor se han fundido.

Love in Music

Though the theme may be the same
Each love has its own song
Which sounds anew in many
Different variations.

One has Spring in his eyes,
Another Summer in his skin,
Or so at least the lover thinks.

But each one conceals a hell
Hidden until the moment
Of tears and the cry of pain
That is torn from the heart.

Since they all lead to hell,
You sought from time to time,
With a wistful prudence,
To avoid their paradises.

But, my friend, who can ignore
Music, if he has a good ear,
Or who can spurn desire,
If he has clear eyes to see.

If some are born fools and others
Wise men, you know to whom you
Belong: sing your song unafraid.

And let the melody of it
Fill all your mind and soul,
For if they be born of love
What matter pleasure or pain?

Derek Harris

Lo más frágil es lo que dura

¿Tu mocedad? No es más
Que un olor de azahar

En plazuela a la tarde
Cuando la luz decae

Y algún farol se enciende.
Su perfume lo sientes

Alzarse de un pasado
Ayer tuyo, hoy extraño,

Envolviéndote: aroma
Unico y sin memoria

De todo, sea la sangre,
Amores o amistades

En tu existir primero,
Cuando cualquier deseo

El tiempo pronto iba
A realizarlo un día

De aquel futuro; aroma
Furtivo como sombra,

Moviendo tus sentidos
Con un escalofrío.

It Is Fragile Things that Last

Your youth? It is only a
Smell of orange blossom

In the square at evening
As the light fades away

And the street lamps are lit.
You can feel its perfume

Embrace you, as it rises
From a past, which was yours

Yesterday, and today
Is alien. No more than

A perfume, bringing back
No memory of anything,

Whether of family or
Of love or of friends

In your first existence
When time would one day soon

In that future fulfill
Your every desire.

A perfume as furtive
As a shadow, stirring

Your senses with a cold
Shiver. And you see that

Y ves que es lo más hondo
De tu vivir un poco

De eso que llaman nada
Tantas gentes sensatas:

Un olor de azahar,
Aire. ¿Hubo algo más?

The center of your life
Is a little of what

Sensible people call
Nothing: the smell of

Orange blossom. Air.
Was there anything else?

Derek Harris

POEMAS PARA UN CUERPO

Sombra de mi

Bien sé yo que esta imagen
Fija siempre en la mente
No eres tú, sino sombra
Del amor que en mí existe
Antes que el tiempo acabe.

Mi amor así visible me pareces,
Por mí dotado de esa gracia misma
Que me hace sufrir, llorar, desesperarme
De todo a veces, mientras otras
Me levanta hasta el cielo en nuestra vida,
Sintiendo las dulzuras que se guardan
Sólo a los elegidos tras el mundo.

Y aunque conozco eso, luego pienso
Que sin ti, sin el raro
Pretexto que me diste,
Mi amor, que afuera está con su ternura,
Allá dentro de mí hoy seguiría
Dormido todavía y a la espera
De alguien que, a su llamada,
Le hiciera al fin latir gozosamente.

Entonces te doy gracias y te digo:
Para esto vine al mundo, y a esperarate;
Para vivir por ti, como tú vives
Por mí, aunque no lo sepas,
Por este amor tan hondo que te tengo.

POEMS FOR A BODY

Shadow of Myself

I know well enough that this image
Fixed for ever in my mind
Is not you, but the shadow
Of love which exists in me
While my time is still not run out.

So you seem to me my love made visible,
Endowed by me with that very grace
Which makes me suffer, weep and despair
Of everything at times, but at others
Lifts me up to the zenith of our life,
Possessing the joys granted only
To the chosen few beyond the world.

And although I know this I then think
That without you, without the rare
Excuse which you gave me, my love,
Now a tenderness outside me,
Would today be there within
Sleeping still and lying in hope
Of someone who, at his call, at last
Would set it beating joyfully.

Then I thank you and say to you;
For this I came into the world, to await you;
To live because of you, as you live
Because of me, even though you do not know it,
Because of this deep love I have for you.

Derek Harris

Haciéndose tarde

Entre los últimos brotes
La rosa no se ve rara,
Ni la alondra al levantarse
Atiende a que el sol retrasa,
O el racimo ya tardío
Cuida si es mustia la parra.
Pero tu cariño nuevo
La estación piensa acabada.

Pues la alondra con su canto
Siempre puebla la mañana
Y la rosa y el racimo
Siempre llenan la mirada,
Entonces, deja, no pienses
En que es tarde. ¿Hubo tardanza
Jamás para olor y zumo
O el revuelo de algún ala?

Fuerza las puertas del tiempo,
Amor que tan tarde llamas.

Getting Late

Among the year's last leaves
The rose is not misplaced,
Nor does the soaring lark
Wait for the tardy sun,
Nor do late-ripened grapes
Care if the vine is spent.
But your new affection
Thinks the season over.

Since the lark always fills
The morning with its song,
And the rose and the grape
Always delight the eye,
Enough then, do not think
It late. Were ever fruit
Or perfume out of season,
Or a bird on the wing?

Break down the doors of time,
Oh love who calls so late.

Derek Harris

Contigo

¿Mi tierra?
Mi tierra eres tú.

¿Mi gente?
Mi gente eres tú.

El destierro y la muerte
Para mí están adonde
No estés tú.

¿Y mi vida?
Dime, mi vida,
¿Qué es, si no eres tú?

With You

My country?
You are my country.

My people?
You are my people.

Exile and death
For me are where
You are not.

And my life?
Tell me, my life,
What is it, if not you?

Anthony Edkins

DESOLACION DE LA QUIMERA

Antes de irse

Más no pedí de ti,
Tú mundo sin virtud,
Que en el aire y en mí
Un pedazo de azul.

A otros la ambición
De fortuna y poder;
Yo sólo quise ser
Con mi luz y mi amor.

THE DISCONSOLATE CHIMERA

Before Leaving

I asked no more of you,
World, world without virtue,
Than a patch of blue
In the sky and in me.

Ambition for fortune and power
Is for others not for me;
I only wanted to be
With my light and my love.

Anthony Edkins

Luis de Baviera escucha *Lohengrin*

Sólo dos tonos rompen la penumbra:
Destellar de algún oro y estridencia granate.
Al fondo luce la caverna mágica
Donde unas criaturas, ¿de qué naturaleza?, pasan
Melodiosas, manando de sus voces música
Que, con fuente escondida, lenta fluye
O, crespa luego, su caudal agita
Estremeciendo el aire fulvo de la cueva
Y con iris perlado riela en notas.

Sombras la sala de auditorio nulo.
En el palco real un elfo solo asiste
Al festejo del cual razón parece dar y enigma:
Negro pelo, ojos sombríos que contemplan
La gruta luminosa, en pasmo friolento
Esculpido. La pelliza de martas le agasaja
Abierta a una blancura, a seda que se anuda en lazo.
Los ojos entornados escuchan, beben la melodía
Como una tierra seca absorbe el don del agua.

Asiste a doble fiesta: una exterior, aquella
De que es testigo; otra interior allá en su mente,
Donde ambas se funden (como color y forma
Se funden en un cuerpo), componen una misma delicia.
Así, razón y enigma, el poder le permite
A solas escuchar las voces a su orden concertadas,
El brotar melodioso que le acuna y nutre
Los sueños, mientras la escena desarrolla,
Ascua litúrgica, una amada leyenda.

Ludwig of Bavaria Listens to *Lohengrin*

Only two colors escape the shadows:
A gleam of gold and a scarlet stridence.
Behind shines the magic cave
Where creatures of some enigmatic species
Move and sing; the music of their voices,
Welling up from a hidden source, calmly
Flows or, with swirling turbulence,
Shakes the tawny air in the cave with notes
Cascading in an iridescent spectrum.

The empty auditorium is in darkness.
In the royal box only an elf watches
The entertainment whose riddle and cause he seems to be:
Black hair, dark eyes gazing at the bright-lit
Grotto, stock-still with cold amazement.
The coat trimmed with sable caresses him
And opens to reveal the whiteness of a silk bow.
His half-closed eyes listen, drinking in the melody
As thirsting land absorbs the gift of water.

He sees a double performance; one outside, the one
He is attending; the other within, there in his mind,
Where both combine (as form and color combine
together in a body) and become one delight.
And so power allows him, the riddle and the cause,
To listen alone to the voices singing at his command.
The melody's flow embraces him, nourishing
His dreams, while the stage displays,
In a sacred glow, a much-loved legend.

Ni existe el mundo, ni la presencia humana
Interrumpe el encanto de reinar en sueños.
Pero, mañana, chambelán, consejero, ministro,
Volverán con demandas estúpidas al rey:
Que gobierne por fin, les oiga y les atienda.
¿Gobernar? ¿Quién gobierna en el mundo de los sueños?
¿Cuándo llegará el día en que gobiernen los lacayos?
Se interpondrá un biombo, benéfico, entre el rey y sus ministros.
Un elfo corre libre los bosques, bebe el aire.

Esa es la vida, y trata fielmente de vivirla:
Que le dejen vivirla. No en la ciudad, el nido
Ya está sobre las cimas nevadas de las sierras
Más altas de su reino. Carretela, trineo,
Por las sendas; flotilla nívea, por los ríos y lagos,
Le esperan siempre, prestos a levantarle
Adonde vive su reino verdadero, que no es de este mundo:
Donde el sueño le espera, donde la soledad le aguarda,
Donde la soledad y el sueño le ciñen su única corona.

Mas la presencia humana es a veces encanto,
Encanto imperioso que el rey mismo conoce
Y sufre con tormento inefable: el bisel de una boca,
Unos ojos profundos, una piel soleada,
Gracia de un cuerpo joven. El lo conoce,
Sí, lo ha conocido, y cuántas veces padecido,
El imperio que ejerce la criatura joven,
Obrando sobre él, dejándole indefenso,
Ya no rey, sino siervo de la humana hermosura.

The world does not exist, nor does a human presence
Disturb the enchantment of reigning in dreams.
But tomorrow chamberlain, adviser, minister,
Will return to the king with their stupid demands:
That he should govern now, take heed and listen to them.
Govern? Who governs in the world of dreams?
When will come the day when lackeys will govern?
A kindly screen will separate king and ministers.
An elf runs free through the woods, drinks in the air.

This is his life, and he tries faithfully to live it:
They should let him live it. Not in the city;
His place is on his kingdom's highest snowy peaks.
A carriage or sledge on the forest-paths,
A snow-white flotilla on river and lake,
Always await him, eager to carry him up to where
Exists his true kingdom, which is not of this world:
Where his dream awaits him, where his solitude is waiting,
Where his solitude and his dream are his only crown.

But a human presence is at times an enchantment,
An imperious enchantment that the king himself knows
And suffers with ineffable torment: the curve of a mouth,
A pair of deep-set eyes, a sun-lit skin,
The grace of a young body. He knows it,
Yes, he has known it, and suffered so often
The power that youth commands,
Subduing him, leaving him defenseless,
No longer a king but a slave to human beauty.

Flotando sobre música el sueño ahora se encarna:
Mancebo todo blanco, rubio, hermoso, que llega
Hacia él y que es él mismo. ¿Magia o espejismo?
¿Es posible a la música dar forma, ser forma de mortal alguno?
¿Cuál de los dos es él, o no es él, acaso, ambos?
El rey no puede, ni aun pudiendo quiere dividirse a sí del otro.
Sobre la música inclinado, como extraño contempla
Con emoción gemela su imagen desdoblada
Y en éxtasis de amor y melodía queda suspenso.

El es el otro, desconocido hermano cuyo existir jamás creyera
Ver algún día. Ahora ahí está y en él ya ama
Aquello que en él mismo pretendieron amar otros.
Con su canto le llama y le seduce. Pero, ¿puede
Consigo mismo unirse? Teme que, si respira, el sueño escape.
Luego un terror le invade: ¿no muere aquel que ve a su doble?
La fuerza del amor, bien despierto ya en él, alza su escudo
Contra todo temor, debilidad, desconfianza.
Como Elsa, ama, mas sin saber a quién. Sólo sabe que ama.

En el canto, palabra y movimiento de los labios
Del otro le habla también el canto, palabra y movimiento
Que a brotar de sus labios al mismo tiempo iban,
Saludando al hermano nacido de su sueño, nutrido por su sueño.
Mas no, no es eso: es la música quien nutriera a su sueño, le dio
forma.
Su sangre se apresura en sus venas, al tiempo apresurando:
El pasado, tan breve, revive en el presente,
Con luz de dioses su presente ilumina al futuro.
Todo, todo ha de ser como su sueño le presagia.

Floating on the music the dream is now made flesh:
A white, blond, beautiful youth, who stands
Beside him, and is himself. Is it magic or mirage?
Can music be given form, be the form of a mortal being?
Which of the two is he, or is he not, perhaps, both?
The king cannot, nor would he, part himself from the other.
Gazing down into the music, like a stranger
He looks with twin emotion on his reflected self,
And in an ecstasy of love and music is entranced.

He is the other one, the unknown brother whose existence
He never thought to see. Now here he is, and in him
He now loves what in himself others claimed to love.
With his song he beckons and seduces him. But can he
Unite himself with himself? He fears that if he breathes
The dream will vanish. Then panic attacks him:
Do not those who see their double die? The strength of love,
Now wide awake in him, raises its shield
Against all fear, weakness and mistrust.
Like Elsa, he loves without knowing whom. He only knows he
loves.

In the song, words and movements of the other's lips
Speak to him also the song, words and movements
That were about to spring from his own lips,
Greeting the brother born of his dream, nourished by his dream.
But no, this is not so: the music fed his dream, gave it form.
His blood quickens in his veins, hastening time:
The past, so brief, relives in the present,
With the light of the gods his present illumines the future.
All, all will be as his dream foretells him.

En el vivir del otro el suyo certidumbre encuentra.
Sólo el amor depara al rey razón para estar vivo,
Olvido a su impotencia, saciedad al deseo
Vago y disperso que tanto tiempo le aquejara.
Se inclina y se contempla en la corriente
Melodiosa e, imagen ajenada, su remedio espera
Al trastorno profundo que dentro de sí siente.
¿No le basta que exista, fuera de él, lo amado?
Contemplar a lo hermoso, ¿no es respuesta bastante?

Los dioses escucharon, y su deseo satisfacen
(Que los dioses castigan concediendo a los hombres
Lo que éstos les piden), y el destino del rey,
Desearse a sí mismo, le trasforma,
Como en flor, en cosa hermosa, inerme, inoperante,
Hasta acabar su vida gobernado por lacayos,
Pero teniendo en ellos, al morir, la venganza de un rey.
Las sombras de sus sueños para él eran la verdad de la vida.
No fue de nadie, ni a nadie pudo llamar suyo.

Ahora el rey está ahí, en su palco, y solitario escucha,
Joven y hermoso, como dios nimbado
Por esa gracia pura e intocable del mancebo,
Existiendo en el sueño imposible de una vida
Que queda sólo en música y que es como música,
Fundido con el mito al contemplarlo, forma ya de ese mito
De pureza rebelde que tierra apenas toca,
Del éter huésped desterrado. La melodía le ayuda a conocerse,
A enamorarse de lo que él mismo es. Y para siempre en la música
vive.

In the other's life his own finds certainty.
Only love gives the king a reason for being alive,
Oblivion to his impotence, satiety to the vague,
Confused desire that has so long pursued him.
Over the melodious waters he leans and gazes,
And, an alien reflection, seeks a remedy
For the disturbance that deep inside him he feels.
Is it not enough that what he loves exists, outside him?
Is not the contemplation of beauty sufficient recompense?

The gods heard, and they satisfy his desire
(For the gods punish men by granting them
What they ask), and the king's destiny,
To desire himself, transforms him into something
As beautiful, vulnerable and useless as a flower,
Until he ends his life governed by lackeys,
But at his death exacting from them a king's vengeance.
The shadows of his dreams were for him the truth of life.
He belonged to no one, nor could he call anyone his own.

Now the king is here, in his box, and alone he listens,
Young and handsome, like a god in the aureole
Of that pure and untouchable grace of youth,
Existing in the impossible dream of life
Found only in music and which is like music,
Fused with the myth he watches, already part of that myth
Of rebel purity, hardly touching the earth,
The aether's exiled guest. The melody helps him to know himself,
To love his real self, and in the music he lives for ever.

Derek Harris

Peregrino

¿Volver? Vuelva el que tenga,
Tras largos años, tras un largo viaje,
Cansancio del camino y la codicia
De su tierra, su casa, sus amigos,
Del amor que al regreso fiel le espere.

Mas ¿tú? ¿Volver? Regresar no piensas,
Sino seguir libre adelante,
Disponible por siempre, mozo o viejo,
Sin hijo que te busque, como a Ulises,
Sin Itaca que aguarde y sin Penélope.

Sigue, sigue adelante y no regreses,
Fiel hasta el fin del camino y tu vida,
No eches de menos un destino más fácil,
Tus pies sobre la tierra antes no hollada,
Tus ojos frente a lo antes nunca visto.

Pilgrim

Return? Let him return who,
After long years and a long journey,
Is weary of the road and homesick for
His land, his home, his friends, the love
Which faithfully awaits his coming.

But for you to return? Don't think of
Going back, but of going freely on,
Young or old, always available,
No son to search for you, like Ulysses,
No waiting Ithaca, and no Penelope.

Go on, go on, and don't go back,
Faithful to the end of the road and life,
Don't hanker for an easier fate,
Your feet on earth not trodden on before,
Your eyes facing the hitherto unseen.

Anthony Edkins

A sus paisanos

No me queréis, lo sé, y que os molesta
Cuanto escribo. ¿Os molesta? Os ofende.
¿Culpa mía tal vez o es de vosotros?
Porque no es la persona y su leyenda
Lo que ahí, allegados a mí, atrás os vuelve.
Mozo, bien mozo era, cuando no había brotado
Leyenda alguna, caísteis sobre un libro
Primerizo lo mismo que su autor: yo, mi primer libro.
Algo os ofende, porque sí, en el hombre y su tarea.

¿Mi leyenda dije? Tristes cuentos
Inventados de mí por cuatro amigos
(¿Amigos?), que jamás quisisteis
Ni ocasión buscasteis de ver si acomodaban
A la persona misma así traspuesta.
Mas vuestra mala fe los ha aceptado.
Hecha está la leyenda, y vosotros, de mí desconocidos,
Respecta al ser que encubre mintiendo doblemente,
Sin otro escrúpulo, a vuestra vez la propaláis.

Contra vosotros y esa vuestra ignorancia voluntaria,
Vivo aún, sé y puedo, si así quiero, defenderme.
Pero aguardáis al día cuando ya no me encuentre
Aquí. Y entonces la ignorancia,
La indiferencia y el olvido, vuestras armas
De siempre, sobre mí caerán, como la piedra,
Cubriéndome por fin, lo mismo que cubristeis
A otros que, superiores a mí, esa ignorancia vuestra
Precipitó en la nada, como al gran Aldana.

To His Countrymen

You don't like me, I know, and all I write
Disturbs you. Disturbs you? It offends you.
Is it my fault perhaps, or is it yours?
Because it's not my personality and the legend
Grown up around it over there that repels you.
While I was still very young, when no legend
Had been formed, you savaged a book
As unfledged as the author himself: me, my first book.
Something offends you, just like that, in the man and his task.

Did I say my legend? Doleful stories
Invented about me by four friends
(Friends?), whom you never liked,
Stories which you never tried to compare
With the person himself disguised by them.
In bad faith you have accepted them.
The legend is formed, and you, unknown to me,
To the man concealed by its double lie, you in your turn
Give it new impetus, without another thought.

Against you and that wilful ignorance of yours,
While I still live, I can and will, if I wish, defend myself.
But you await the day when I am here
No more. And then ignorance,
Indifference and oblivion, your age-old weapons,
Shall fall on me, like the gravestone,
Covering me at last, just as you covered
Others better than I, like the great Aldana,*
Whom that ignorance of yours hurled into the abyss.

* *Aldana:* Francisco de Aldana (1537-1578), a major poet whose work has been unjustly neglected.

De ahí mi paradoja, por lo demás involuntaria,
Pues la imponéis vosotros: en nuestra lengua escribo,
Criado estuve en ella y, por eso, es la mía,
A mi pesar quizá, bien fatalmente. Pero con mis expresas excepciones,
A vuestros escritores de hoy ya no los leo.
De ahí la paradoja: soy, sin tierra y sin gente,
Escritor bien extraño; sujeto quedo aún más que otros
Al viento del olvido que, cuando sopla, mata.

Si vuestra lengua es la materia
Que empleé en mi escribir y, si por eso,
Habréis de ser vosotros los testigos
De mi existencia y su trabajo,
En hora mala fuera vuestra lengua
La mía, la que hablo, la que escribo.
Así podréis con tiempo, como venís haciendo,
A mi persona y mi trabajo echar afuera
De la memoria, en vuestro corazón y vuestra mente.

Grande es mi vanidad, diréis,
Creyendo a mi trabajo digno de la atención ajena
Y acusándoos de no querer la vuestra darle.
Ahí tendréis razón. Mas el trabajo humano
Con amor hecho, merece la atención de los otros,
Y poetas de ahí tácitos lo dicen
Enviando sus versos a través del tiempo y la distancia
Hasta mí, atención demandando.
¿Quise de mí dejar memoria? Perdón por ello pido.

Mas no todos igual trato me dais,
Que amigos tengo aún entre vosotros,
Doblemente queridos por esa desusada
Simpatía y atención entre la indiferencia,
Y gracias quiero darles ahora, cuando amargo
Me vuelvo y os acuso. Grande el número
No es, mas basta para sentirse acompañado
A la distancia en el camino. A ellos
Vaya así mi afecto agradecido.

Here's my paradox, albeit unwilling, since you
Impose it on me: I write in our tongue,
I was raised in it, and so, perhaps to my sorrow,
It is well and truly mine. But with very few exceptions
I never read your writers of today.
Here's the paradox: I am a very strange writer,
Without a country, without a people; subject more than most
To the wind of oblivion, which when it blows, kills.

If your tongue is the material
I used in my writings, and if, because of this,
You are to be the witnesses
Of my existence and its work,
I curse your tongue,
My tongue, the one I speak, the one I write.
So you can, with time, as you are doing now
In your hearts and minds, cast out
From your memory my person and my work.

You may say I am too vain because
I believe my work worthy of others' attention
And accuse you of not wishing to give it yours.
Here you would be right. But a man's work,
Done with love, deserves the attention of others,
And poets from over there tacitly admit this
By sending their verses through time and space
To me, demanding attention from me.
Did I want to leave a memory of myself? Sorry!

But not all of you treat me this way,
I still have some friends amongst you,
Doubly cherished for that unaccustomed
Sympathy and attention amidst indifference,
And I wish to thank them now, when I become
Bitter and attack you. They are not many
But enough to feel oneself accompanied,
At a distance, along the road. To them
Goes therefore my affectionate gratitude.

Acaso encuentre aquí reproche nuevo:
Que ya no hablo con aquella ternura
Confiada, apacible de otros días.
Es verdad, y os lo debo, tanto como
A la edad, al tiempo, a la experiencia.
A vosotros y a ellos debo el cambio. Si queréis
Que ame todavía, devolvedme
Al tiempo del amor. ¿Os es posible?
Imposible como aplacar ese fantasma que de mí evocasteis.

Perhaps I find here a new reproach:
That I no longer speak with that calm,
Trusting tenderness of former days.
It's true, and the fault is yours, as much as that
Of age, time and experience.
To you and to these I owe the change. If you want
Me to love still, take me back to
The time of love. Can you?
No more than you can placate that phantom you made of me.

Derek Harris

RITTER LIBRARY
BALDWIN-WALLACE COLLEGE